"With unflinching honesty, Bonnie Keen guides 'bent, broken, and bedraggled' men and women everywhere *(and aren't we all there at sometime in life?)* out from the depths of depression and unabashedly draws them to The One who offers light, grace, and hope, no matter where they find themselves along the way."

—Julie Ann Barnhill,
bestselling author of *She's Gonna Blow!, Scandalous Grace, Radical Forgiveness,* and *Exquisite Hope*

"Recognizing this malady as a disease and not a spiritual shortcoming is, in my opinion, an important and pivotal theme—and Bonnie's insight on this matter is a refreshing breeze from heaven...I highly recommend this one."

—Michael Omartian,
record producer and composer

"The dark, murky swamp of depression is difficult to navigate for anyone who finds herself or himself lost there. Bonnie Keen knows this well. She has lived there...But there is a way out. Bonnie is a trustworthy guide—eloquent, bright, compelling, and compassionate as she speaks of her journey and encourages others on theirs."

—Jan Silvious,
speaker, author of *Big Girls Don't Whine* and *Foolproofing Your Life*

"With a rare combination of vulnerability, gut-level honesty, and wisdom from the experts, Bonnie Keen allows the reader to experience her journey from hopeless depression to resurrection and a future. This book grabbed my heart and forced me to confront my own journey through the valley, and gave me a tool for personal and ministry use. Don't miss it!"

—Carol Kent,
speaker, author of *When I Lay My Isaac Down*

"As a speaker and a 'listener,' I'm finding that women are coming apart at the seams in great numbers. The culprit is depression. I'm often at a loss for words on this gut-sucking crisis. This book, *A Ladder out of Depression*, not only gives me answers, but it's a resource I can recommend wholeheartedly to those in despair. It's a book of hope!"

—Sue Buchanan,
author, speaker, cheerleader!

"Bonnie's message is clear...God will meet you right where you are, take you by the hand, and walk you through life's darkest hour—He will show you how to live again! It is not by coincidence this book is in your hand—don't miss out on this life-changing message!"

—Nancy Alcorn,
author, and founder of
Mercy Ministries of America

"Whether you are suffering from depression or want to reach out to someone who is, this is a priceless resource that will most definitely bring His light into the deepest darkness."

—Kathy Troccoli,
singer, author, speaker

"*A Ladder out of Depression* offers a word in season to the 'often in denial' body of Christ by giving us a real, vulnerable, and hopeful resource to encourage us in life's blistery moments."

—Chris Williamson,
Senior Pastor,
Strong Tower Bible Church,
Franklin, Tennessee

A LADDER OUT OF DEPRESSION

BONNIE KEEN

HARVEST HOUSE PUBLISHERS
EUGENE, OREGON

Cover by Left Coast Design, Portland, Oregon

Cover image © Chris Cheadle/Photographer's Choice/Getty Images

This book is not intended to take the place of sound medical advice or to treat specific maladies. Neither the author nor the publisher assumes any liability for possible adverse consequences as a result of the information contained herein. Readers are advised to consult with their physician or other medical practitioner before implementing any suggestion that follows.

A LADDER OUT OF DEPRESSION
Copyright © 2005 by Bonnie Keen
Published by Harvest House Publishers
Eugene, Oregon 97402

Library of Congress Cataloging-in-Publication Data
  Keen, Bonnie, 1955–
    A ladder out of depression / Bonnie Keen.
        p. cm.
    ISBN-13: 978-0-7369-1531-1 (pbk.)
    ISBN-10: 0-7369-1531-1 (pbk.)
    1. Depression, Mental—Religious aspects—Christianity. 2. Keen, Bonnie, 1955–
  I. Title.
    BV4910.34.K44 2005
    248.8'625—dc22   2005001898

Printed in the United States of America

05   06   07   08   09   10   11   12   / VP-CF /   10   9   8   7   6   5   4   3

To my great-aunt Helen

Thank you for the clear whispers of truth
into my darkest moments.

ACKNOWLEDGMENTS

Heart Above Water

How can I truly thank the people who saved my life over and over again when depression tried to take me out? How is it possible to honor the following friendships and relationships—pastoral, medical, full of wisdom and grace? My heart remains above water because of the love in motion from Russ and Tori Taff, Max Lucado, Scotty Smith, Dr. David McMillan, Dr. Burton Sanders, Donna Goldman, Carlana Harwell, Dale Hanson Bourke, and Nancy Alcorn; from my mom, Gwendolyn; my daddy, Fred; my sister, Amy; and my brother, Stan.

Great-aunt Helen, this book was written to honor you.

Harvest House Publishers' Terry Glaspey and Carolyn McCready kept me on the path of birthing this book when I came up against moments too painful to push through. Paul Gossard and Terry put the pieces of the manuscript together with great care and skill.

To the ones I touch, cry with, and pray for—the beloved, suffering new friends I am meeting: I thank you for inspiring me to write about my personal struggle with depression. This is my offering of hope to you.

To my husband, Brent: I adore you for loving me with respect and ongoing compassion. Courtney and Graham, you are my very heartbeat, and you kept me alive more times than you will ever know.

The greatest gift I can give all of you is to keep my heart above water, to thank you by walking in recovery, and to glorify God for His gift of love to me through your lives.

Great and glorious God and Thou, Lord Jesus, I pray
Ye shed abroad Your light in the darkness of my mind.

ST. FRANCIS OF ASSISI

CONTENTS

GOD'S GIFT OF HOPE

I am not an expert on the disease of depression.

I have lived through its hell.

I have spoken with many of its victims.

I do believe that in all things, God's light breaks through every darkness. Nothing is wasted.

This book is a tribute to all of us who lament in the valley of Baca—the valley of tears—and to the ones who love us. We are not alone. Depression does not have the final word. May the light of Christ Jesus bring you the gift of hope and banish the fear of darkness from your soul.

PART ONE

FALLING OFF

Men and women who are

truly filled with light are those who have

gazed deeply into the darkness

of their imperfect existence.[1]

~

BRENNAN MANNING
The Ragamuffin Gospel

A Garden Lost,
A Garden Found

Most dogs like to chase cars. But there's a dog in our neighborhood who has turned chasing vehicles into a full-scale Olympic event. We call him "Tripod" because he has only three legs. Please do not give a sympathetic sigh for Tripod. He was born with three legs and has a ragingly fabulous sense of self-esteem. He has absolutely no idea he's handicapped. If he looked in a mirror, I believe he would see a reflection of a pit bull on steroids. Tripod could outrun any canine in the state, as well as most vehicles that cross his path. Terrorizing innocent drivers makes his day.

The first few times the jet-black dog charged straight into the path of my car, I screamed in fear of slamming into him and rendering him a two-legged creature. What it took me a while to understand, though, was his crafty, smug psyche. He has no intention of being hit. At the exact moment of a potential fur-flying demise, he veers out of danger with a glimmer of smiling white teeth. Not once has Mr. T been grazed by the hundreds of tires he's targeted.

Recently Tripod came straight at me. With determination, I kept my eyes focused, stayed on high alert, and refused to slow down. "I know what you're about and I'm not playing this game," I muttered. His bark is far worse than his bite—the apparent onslaught holds little resolve. In the end, Tripod is the coward.

Checking my rearview mirror, however, I noticed an innocent driver behind me. I admit I had to laugh—the scene behind me was like something out of a movie. Tripod must have drooled with excitement as new prey approached. The driver did what all first-timers do. Trying to avoid the crazed three-legged dog, the car swerved from one lane to the other, apparently traumatized... as with all first encounters of the Tripod kind.

This jet-black dog comes out of nowhere, unannounced, and tries with all his might to throw people off track. Literally, physically—and most definitely psychologically—the mad dog attempts to land someone in a ditch.

Depression is very much like Mr. Tripod.

It comes like a black monster at those of us who suffer from its threats. Depression takes most of us by utter surprise.

Like a crazed dog, depression can wreck our lives. The symptoms are uniquely similar: quiet, stillness—disrupted by a bark so loud, so frightening, it shuts out sanity and hope. Depression's lies send adrenaline-laden toxic fear rushing through the healthiest of hearts.

We might be thrown off course for a time.

Yet help is here.

Depression does not define us.

We have access to help in every area, help that's three-pronged just like Mr. Tripod: Physical, emotional, and spiritual healing is waiting to be drawn in as balm for the hopeless, despairing soul.

We were made to walk in a garden, full of grace and truth, breezes blowing, hand-in-hand in relationship with the Creator of the universe.

Made by Him, Made for Him

There is so much we were not created to know!

We were made to walk in a garden, full of grace and truth, breezes blowing, hand-in-hand in relationship with the Creator of the universe, without shame, fear, or despair.

"In the beginning" we were made as God's children to live in harmony, protected by a Father who can deal with good and evil and everything in between.

Man and woman were made in the image of God, with one major exception.

We were not made to understand evil. We were not equipped to go head-to-head with the Tripods of this world.

Tragically, Adam and Eve opened Pandora's box. They were instructed to indulge in the fruit of every tree in Eden except the tree of "good and evil."[2] God wasn't playing games. He so loved them that He was looking out for them as a parent does a child. Man and woman were not wired to comprehend good and evil.

This particular tree bore fruit only God could handle. He alone can wrestle down the devil and fight battles we cannot understand. Humans fail miserably in this arena. God has been rescuing us ever since we barrelled into scenes we weren't written into.

Humans were created to love, laugh, and enjoy good things as innocent children before our Creator. We were given access to all the beauty this world has to offer. Love, marriage, food, endless variations of nature, breathtakingly simple moments of rest, silence; the laughter of our children, stunningly delightful animals; the possessions of the earth have all been our inheritance from the beginning of time.

Emotionally, physically, and spiritually we were not wired to deal with rape, disease, injustice, torment, prejudice, divorce, terrorism…or depression!

We were created for a garden. Although the original Garden was corrupted, God has made a way back to Him, to His protection and healing through the gift of His Son. A new garden waits for us, bought by the blood of Christ.

It took the death of God's heart to break new ground.

The original dream refuses to die.

Loved by Him

I cannot quite get over the image from the movie *The Passion of the Christ* in which Mary interacts with her beaten, bloodied son. For a moment, He falls to the ground, and Mary finds the courage to rush to His side. The love-stained eyes of Jesus look into his mother's, and He speaks the prophetic words from Isaiah, "Behold, mother, I make all things new." Wrapped up in this promise, spoken through the broken teeth of a face barely recognizable, we hear in his pain the echo of every child's plea: "Mother, look at me! Look what I can do!" And He breaks our hearts.

I've suffered with clinical depression for more than ten years now and am convinced more than ever that I will not allow depression to come roaring into my soul again like Tripod on steroids.

Too much was given by Christ Jesus for me to give up.

Too much was overcome for me to be overcome.

Yes, there is a new garden to be fully realized, a time when depression will be down for the count and truly out.

Today, God isn't offended by the broken heart.

His love is all about hope in the most dire, ugly, and dark places.

God's love showed up for me in the prayers of friends, godly advice, and medication from skilled doctors' observations. Love, truth, and pieces of hope pulled me out of the pit at the end of my ladder. In sharing my journey and the experiences of others who have successfully made it through this challenge, I know the Lord God will meet you wherever you are.

Depression has been defeated.

Embrace the defeat!

Reach out and hold onto the ladder of God's truth and provision that will lead you up into the light.

A new garden is waiting.

~

This seems a cheerful world...when I view it from this fair garden...But if I climbed some great mountain and looked out...you know very well what I would see; brigands on the high road, pirates on the seas, in the amphitheatres men murdered to please the applauding crowds . . .

Yet in spite of it, I have found a quiet and holy people... They are despised and persecuted, but they care not. They have overcome the world. These people...are Christians.

ST. CYPRIAN

writing to his friend Donatus (third century)

The thing which I greatly feared is come upon me,

and that which I was afraid of is come unto me.

I was not in safety, neither had I rest,

neither was I quiet, yet trouble came.

~

THE WORDS OF JOB

2

MENTAL MELTDOWN

M ommy, are you going to die?" My ten-year-old daughter's question shot through a foggy, exhausted, gray-lined haze.

"No, Courtney—why would you say such at thing?"

"You act like you're dying." Courtney was never one to mince words. "I just want to know." Her brave, one-eyed-squinting, don't-mess-with-me attitude masked what I knew was a fear-filled little girl's heart.

With a mother's naïve wish, I had hoped my children would perhaps ignore the symptoms of my clinical depression. But my lack of sleep, extreme weight loss, and constant flow of tears were not lost on the wise-eyed older one.

It was time to confront the truth.

Thankfully, words came to me from a Father, a God of strength and mercy who I had depended on through the years of divorce, single parenthood, and now the confusion of a mental meltdown.

Gathering Courtney and her younger brother, Graham, on the couch, I took a deep breath and looked into their faces. *(They've been through enough already, Lord,* I mumbled to myself. *Now they have to see me fall apart?*) We sat in the den, our favorite place to build a fire or watch movies, a room where they would perform skits and plays for me. Our home might have been described as "broken" by some, but the three of us knew the laughter and joy we had together, determined to build new traditions through a bond of fierce love and loyalty.

Now, after drudging through the aftermath of divorce…bills stacked high, a loss of my life work, poor dating choices…the once resilient mother had hit a wall.

"You know, when you guys are sick with the flu or an infection, we have to call the doctor and get medicine," I began. "I put you on the couch here and let you stay home from school to get well." Sitting in my bathrobe, red-eyed, void of energy, with a cloud of despair almost palpable in the room, I tried to smile. (*Should I bring up Popsicles, ice cream, and treats handed out without caution as a poor analogy for the medication I've begun?* I wondered.) Christmas lights were blinking, and the house was decorated for celebration. Now, my children needed some kind of assurance that their mother was going to be a part of this holiday, their favorite of the year—I was the rock in their young lives and the rock was presently cracking.

A nod of my children's heads let me know they were beginning to understand my explanation of clinical depression in "kid-speak."

"Well, my feelings sort of have the flu," I finished.

Graham, six years old at the time, listened with more curiosity than did his older sister, whose green eyes seared into mine with a warning of *Give me truth and nothing but the truth so help us all, Mommy dearie.*

"My heart is not feeling well. But I have doctors helping me and people praying for me to get well. If I cry, don't worry—it's not your fault. I'm going to be all right." I tried to sound convincing. "Everything is going to be all right. I just need a little time to feel strong again."

As usual I followed my speech with a gathering of my babes into my arms for kisses and hugs, breathing in the enchanting smells of their being. I had given the best description I could for the terrifying condition I found myself in at Christmas of 1995. *Clinical depression.* Doctors had warned me I should be hospitalized, and my defiant refusal was confirmed by the pair of eyes that looked to me as the center of their world. I would not be in a hospital, especially during Christmas, or any other time for that matter.

The thought *What would Mother Teresa do?* oddly went through my mind.

Who knows? She was as tough as nails, full of grace, yet she even suffered her own seasons of depression. Would anyone understand my meltdown?

I was determined to face the battle of depression, and by God's grace, learn to understand and fight this uninvited but undeniable breakdown.

The anxiety of wanting to die, the feelings of hopelessness, the emotions all over the map, allowed a free fall without a net... into a bed of mercy.

Jewels of Survival

The word *depression* comes from the Latin *deprimere,* which translates literally "to press down." In the first few weeks of clinical depression I felt not only as if I were being pressed down, but as if I were being crushed and left gasping for air.

As a broken-down, basket-case child of God, somewhere in my guts I knew the Spirit of God was being crushed along with me. Strange concept. As I was being pressed, so was the Creator of the world, who resided in my heart. And as God's love was compressed, distilled, and pressurized, an amazing miracle was taking place.

Less of me, more of Him, less of my self-sufficiency, more of redemption.

It wasn't pretty. But it worked.

This was not quite the "diamond in the rough" chipping away I had imagined. Yet the anxiety of wanting to die, the feelings of hopelessness, the emotions all over the map, allowed a free fall without a net…into a bed of mercy.

God's love for me survived the darkness. Not only survived the darkness, but became the light in my fall from reality, a light that drew me even more closely to Him. This light allowed me to seek medical help and counseling, not just relying on prayer but embracing the practical sources of recovery without shame.

What neither my children nor I knew that Christmas when I sat trembling, holding them and speaking forced reassurances, was that a new treasure waited for us. Love pressed into the darkness with me, and a grace-ravaged gem was being formed.

Depression appeared to hold the pen that would write the last chapter in my story. As my eyes grew accustomed to the dark, there flickered the light of never-before-seen horizons—promises of new hope. Depression seemed the last straw for me. My emotional back was broken, I was down for the count. But my emotional back at last showed me the truth of who I was…and a clearer picture of my humanity, desperate for a Savior.

Now I pray for you who suffer with this disease that you will believe what I can now say with all confidence: You *can* and *will* recover. You are not alone! Depression has been around since the beginning of time and is presently being treated with the greatest degree of success in human history.

As you grow stronger in your unique and individual way, watch for the jewels of survival that will be formed by the crushing in your heart. They are priceless places that will one day allow you to feel more deeply, love more passionately, and extend more compassion to other hurting ones.

If I were reading this in the early days of my depression, I might have thrown this book across the room. But the next line written here may have stopped me. For, know that I know that eventually a smile may light on your face, an unsuspected butterfly kissing your cheeks. In spite of the pain, in spite of your doubt, in spite of the disease of depression, God will never let go of you until you are through the darkness and are able to believe again in the strength of His light.

. . . As all the Heavens were a Bell,

And Being but an Ear,

And I and Silence some strange Race

Wrecked, solitary, here——

And then a Plank in Reason, broke,

And I dropped down, and down——

And hit a World, at every plunge,

And Finished knowing——then——

~

EMILY DICKINSON,
from "I Felt a Funeral in my Brain"

3

DOWN THE RABBIT'S HOLE

A "plank in reason broke" for me on a national tour, while I was singing with recording artists I enjoyed, in arenas filling with upwards of 10,000 people. Clueless as to why my mind spiraled out of control, I felt like Alice free-falling down the rabbit's hole. Rooms were too large, sleep was a fantasy, food tasted alien, and no one seemed to speak the same language.

My emotions pitched forward into darkness while I was invited onto a platform each evening to sing about the miracle of Christmas. A celebration of the Christ Child! The tour experience seemed a cruel mockery. How could I possibly sing the words of Handel's Messiah, the "Hallelujah Chorus," with Death breathing down my neck?

The one great cosmetic girl-trick I discovered was the ability to cry for hours and maintain my "face." Before going onto the platform, allowing my eyes to fill up with tears, I would wait until the last second then lean straight over into a jackknife stance, blinking hard so that the tears fell straight down to the floor. With a deliberate swing of the head back upright, my makeup would survive relatively intact. Then onto the platform I would walk, singing to a sea of glittering holiday sweaters and smiling faces.

The audience was a vista of children and families. Everywhere I turned was a portrait of what I longed for and did not believe I would ever experience: a whole family. Depression transformed what would normally have been a beautiful setting into a stinging joke.

My life was a mess.

Divorce, single parenthood, and now this. This—molasses in my veins, a venom-in-my-heart curse that was taking over my mind and body—what was this?

I couldn't eat. And I love to eat.

I couldn't sleep. And usually on tour I slept more than usual. On this tour, I slept for two hours at a time and then was awake, tortured by thoughts of loss, despair, hopelessness, more loss, pain, tears, more tears, more pain, and now sloppy mascara marks everywhere.

Prayer didn't help.

Advice from the best friends in the world fell flat.

The faces of my children…they might keep me alive.

But for what?

For more years of financial debt? For more years of trying to make sense out of a lost ministry? For more years of dating and saying "yes" to men that meant well but were not right for me… For more years of pushing through a wall of aching, pain-ridden faith in what?

Did I still believe in God?

DID I HAVE THE COURAGE to hope?

I had white-knuckled my way through a divorce, moving ahead with all the grace I could muster for my ex-husband and his new wife. My children hadn't dropped out of school or turned into beastly apparitions of defeat. They were doing well and putting up with their mom's disastrous dating scenarios.

My Achilles' heel…I was ever the royal wreck when it came to men. A wilting sense of myself as an unappealing woman, mixed with vintage guilt bred into my bones. Guilt and fear of failure were mother's milk to me. This toxic emotional recipe was topped off with a whopping certainty that I deserved nothing. Consequently, I attempted to settle for almost any possibility that came my way. The horror of an attempted date rape and several broken engagements littered the years after my divorce.

In the bleak midwinter of my breakdown, my mind was reeling, spinning, thinking, rethinking, questioning, hurting… hurting…hurting…until pain became my only reality.

The rest of the world could have Christmas!

I wanted out!

But there was no out!

DAYS OFF ON THE TWO-WEEK "holiday" tour were sheer agony.

My mind would fall further down into the monster rabbit's hole.

Lock the door, ask for room service if anything sounds edible, don't think, yes, think, pray, no, can't pray…just make sure no one sees this…make sure to be alone. Crying for hours, I lay with a Bible open against my heart, begging God for some kind of relief. Stinging silence crushed my prayers.

Then I tried another approach. I'd punch God in the face!

"I find it incredibly hard to believe You could love me and let me hurt this much!" I screamed at God into the pillow so no one but *He* could hear.

Still, silence upon silence.

Such a series of silent nights.

A journal entry of mine from this time says it all:

> This morning I had thoughts of death again, of how, if I didn't have my children, I might just long to be with God. Maybe what I'm saying is that I don't want to face what God is requiring of me here in this world. I just

don't want to hurt anymore. His ways are not mine, but His ways seem so hard. When I think of all the men and women in the Bible called to a special walk with God, and what was asked of them, I want to cry out, "I CANNOT HANDLE THIS! I CANNOT DO THIS! YOU'RE ASKING TOO MUCH!"

But was God asking anything more of me?

No.

I was in a clinical depression and losing grip on reality. The diagnosis would not come until I was off the tour, off the road, home again.

Until then, however, the free fall picked up speed.

WHEN AT LAST THE CITIES and concerts were finished, I was emotionally, physically, and spiritually wrung out. I sat like a zombie in the front of the tour bus as it pulled into my hometown in the wee hours of the morning. Could I drive home? How would I function? It was as if the marrow of my very soul had been drained off into an unseen, ravenous blackness.

A friend of mine, suffering after the suicide of her husband, wrote of her first stage of depression:

> I didn't faint or lose consciousness. I just felt numb all over. The pace of my thoughts and actions was greatly reduced, as if I were moving in slow motion. There was a fuzziness, a blurring of all that was going on, like I was walking through a fog. Feelings of helplessness overwhelmed me...My appetite vanished as my own body system went into defensive reaction. I found it hard to concentrate, and I lost my thoughts in the middle of a sentence. Confusion ruled my mind.[1]

I would have paid big bucks for a fainting spell, for anything that would knock me flat out of commission.

Jack Nicholson's plight in the movie *One Flew Over the*

Cuckoo's Nest rushed into my mind. His Oscar-winning character was a depressed man, right? He was given shock treatments, stared out barred windows, and went mad. And the people around him had names like "Nurse Ratchet." Was this because depressed people are the ultimate failures? This was the closest acquaintance I had with depression. Of course, there was also the closing scene in the Francis Farmer movie, where she was given a lobotomy!

Too many movies, too little knowledge, too much panic, not enough fight.

THE LEGALISTIC VOICES OF MY PAST whispered lethal discouragement from recesses of my consciousness: *If only you had more faith, you wouldn't be in this shape. If you were praying the right prayers, and weren't such a screw up…if you were more of something…if you could hold it together…if you knew Christ more…if, if, if…guilt…despair…loss…*

By the time I made it to the office of my pastor I was 20 pounds thinner, not a great look for me, and shaking from head to toe. The morning Scotty Smith opened his door that cold December day there was no pretence of proper etiquette. Shuddering, weeping, extremely underweight and terrified, I shamelessly begged him for help.

I had entered the land of full-blown clinical depression and for the first time in my life, I faced the fight of my life, a literal fight for life itself.

PART TWO

GETTING A GRIP

The growth of understanding

follows an ascending spiral

rather than a straight line.

~

JOANNA FIELD

4

NAME THIS DISEASE

Everyone has a ladder to climb in this life. The ladder represents our passions—what gets our juices flowing, the places of pleasure and joy we choose to keep us climbing up and on. Sure, it's up a few steps and then down a couple and back up again... that's life. The strength of the ladder lies in what it's made of.

What happens to a person of faith—a person who believes God wants only good for them and their children, family, or future—when the ladder begins to sway and the impossible happens? How do you cope with shattered dreams, deaths of covenants, loss of life, cancer, financial chaos...betrayals, addiction? Doesn't Jeremiah 29:11 promise that God has a future and hope to prosper and not harm His beloved? What happens when the last rung on the ladder breaks and you fall into depression?

For a person whose ladder is grounded on faith in Jesus Christ and the love of an all-powerful God, such a ladder has a grave test to withstand! If you suffer with depression, a theological earthquake will shake you; the ground will yawn open and threaten to swallow up every last inch of you.

In certain seasons, life can feel like a long January, as Brennan Manning puts it. The promises of God sound cruel. The distance between man and God, from the world of loss we live in to the Creator, seems too far, too hard, too difficult to reach across.

What happens when the shielding around our hearts begins to leak, the rain floods in, the floors rust, and the ladder crumbles?

Choose to Understand

> Yes, if you cry out for insight and raise your voice for understanding, if you seek...Wisdom as for hidden treasures, then you will...find the knowledge of...God.[1]

I don't intend to overwhelm anyone reading this book with the statistics about depression. It you're suffering from depression, all you can think about is your own pain and how to get out of the blackness that surrounds your life. Perhaps, however, in looking at some of the symptoms and facts we know about the disease, you can see that you are not an aberration. You are not imagining things; you most certainly are not alone.

"Depression is partly in our genes, partly in our childhood experience, partly in our way of thinking, partly in our brains, partly in our way of handling emotions."[2] It feels overwhelming because it literally affects every area of our being.

Crying is an unavoidable symptom of depression. Tears from depression flow from a seemingly endless spring of pain. Charlie Brown said, "Adversity is what makes you mature. The growing soil is watered best by tears of sadness."[3] Our tears have much to teach us about who we are. Crying out for understanding is a necessary first step back up the ladder.

Depression must be understood to be overcome. Understanding what was happening to me was vitally important to any recovery and for finding the strength to climb my ladder again.

WHAT IS depression? I had to name this monster, and I learned to choke out the words *disease—mental disease*. Could it possibly be true I was dealing with a mental disorder?

Yes.

I detested this terminology but reluctantly admitted I was in the throes of a serious clinical, chemical, and genetic depression. I had a *disease*—or as Webster's dictionary terms it, "a serious, active, prolonged, and deep-rooted condition." Thank you.

There was a small sense of relief in naming the culprit. In my early stages of wrestling with the "black dog sitting at my heels"—Winston Churchill's words—I exhaled a bit and found that depression is as old as the earth itself. Life in the Garden didn't equip any of us to deal with loss. Life out of the Garden is filled with loss, and loss is the root of the majority of depressive episodes—loss, and genetic and chemical imbalances of the brain brought on by a myriad of catalysts.

Around 2400 years ago, the Greek doctor Hippocrates spoke of "melancholia," explaining that a depression was literally caused by "black, heavy blood passing through the patient's veins." The Greeks believed that depression was caused by too much "black bile" in the blood.[4] Oh yes, this rang true for me. There were moments when I doubted that my heart would be able to beat through its heavy blood for another day or night…or even if it was worth the effort. It's understandable that thousands of years ago, a diagnosis of depression would be based in vivid cardiac imagery.

Thankfully, we live in a time that offers a much broader view of this disease in its varying forms, and most importantly, there is much that can be done to get the bloodflow back to normal.

The Unknown

Job writes in the oldest book of the Bible of his own despair, the words of a righteous man of God enduring loss after loss, physically, spiritually, and emotionally:

> If I go to the east, God is not there;
> If I go to the west, I do not see him.
> When he is at work in the north, I catch no sight of him;
> When he turns to the south, I cannot see him.[5]

Depression blocks out anything but darkness. It's as if someone placed a filter over the heart's eyes that allows only the sense of defeat, loss, and hopelessness to seep through. As Anaïs Nin wrote, "We don't see things as they are, we see them as we are."

On the Web site for the Cleveland Clinic, depression is defined in simplistic terms: "Being depressed is a normal reaction to loss, life's struggles, or an injured self-esteem. But sometimes the feelings of sadness become intense, lasting for long periods of time and preventing a person from leading a normal life."[6]

No kidding! How about "being depressed is a violent reaction to loss and to life, filled with unknown seasons of intense doubt." It waits like a three-legged dog in one's DNA for just the right moment to erupt as a chemical imbalance and throw one to the ground. As for lasting "long periods of time," it took more than a year for me to even get back to normal. For the rest of my life, I may face depressive episodes. Yet now I am armed with knowledge of what I'm dealing with, and how to keep this disease from eroding my life.

World-renowned author William Styron wrote of his bout with depression in his book, *Darkness Visible*. This brilliant master of language refers to the word *depression* as a "simply inadequate expression of the experience—a true wimp of a word for such a major illness."[7]

If you're someone who suffers with depression or have a family or friend you are trying to love through this disease, you are not alone. It's a disorder that continues to plague, baffle, and leave many speechless.

↪

This is some of what we do know about depression.

Worldwide, depression is believed to affect more than 300 million people. According to the National Institute of Mental Health, nearly 18.8 million Americans over the age of 18 suffer from major depression. Some sources state that 3 percent of

Americans—19 million—suffer from chronic depression. More than 2 million of these are cases involving children. Manic–depressive conditions, in which a person's mood swings violently from extreme highs to extreme lows, afflict close to 2.3 million people, and are listed as the second-leading killer of young women, the third-leading killer of young men.[8] Andrew Solomon puts it this way in his book *The Noonday Demon:*

> Depression claims more years than war, cancer, and AIDS put together. Other illnesses, from alcoholism to heart disease, mask depression when it causes them; if one takes that into consideration, depression may be the biggest killer on earth.[9]

Suicide is the third-largest cause of death in 10- to 24-year-olds, and in the elderly. There are 55,000 such incidents documented annually, but the true statistics are closer to 100,000. One out of every 200 people suffering from depression will eventually commit suicide.[10]

Unfortunately, many people do not seek treatment. Left untreated, depression can last for years, causing untold torment, and needless wasted years and loss of life. Far too many people live hanging on by their fingernails, ashamed, afraid to reveal their despair in spite of the fact they live in a day of the most advanced and enlightened treatment ever available.

Depression in the Church

Depression strikes Christians and non-Christians without discrimination. It's not about race, creed, or financial status—it's "symptomatic of life in an imperfect, fallen world, and it plays no favorites with race, creed or color."[11] Yet depression has a stigma because it's a disease of the mind. It's an elusive disorder that is not easily addressed in any community, especially among people of faith.

While churches are increasingly filled with depressed parishioners, many church leaders are reluctant to address the subject.

It's the unspoken sense of failure attached to depression that keeps many, like myself, reluctant to admit that we need help.

If you are reading along and think that only the weak of faith or faint of heart suffer from depression, then I invite you to explore why some of the greatest people of faith suffer from other diseases and disasters: endless varieties of cancer, forms of addictions, divorce, deaths from Alzheimer's and Parkinson's, infant

> There is beauty and loveliness here on earth, but it's...as impossible to retain as it is to grasp the wind in your hand. Far greater is the truth—the understanding that *depression does not define the end of our story.*

death syndrome, car wrecks. We who believe in Jesus are saved by His blood, but this side of heaven, we are not given a "get-out-of-disease-free" card. We are not immune to the human experience.

> We tend to think life should be fair because God is fair. But God is not life. And if I confuse God with the physical reality of life—by expecting constant good health, for example—then I set myself up for crushing disappointment.[12]

Depression is a disease that steals far too much from far too many. The diseases suffered by Christ on the cross, nailed down and defeated, include *all* torments, both physical and mental.

There is beauty and loveliness here on earth, but it's hard-fought-for, hard-won, and as impossible to retain as it is to grasp the wind in your hand. Far greater is the truth—the understanding that *depression does not define the end of our story.*

Depression may attempt to rob us of our inheritance. Yet as we come to grasp the inner workings of this disease, how it can be treated with biblical truths, medical options, and godly counsel, we can name and tame the monster.

It's not up to you or me to "fix" ourselves.

It *is* up to us to become educated and to believe in the power of God to be with us as we move up the ladder one step at a time.

THERE ARE TWO PLANS GOING ON for your life, suggests Pastor Chris Williamson of Strong Tower Bible Church. Yes, there is the plan in Jeremiah 29:11. God does want good for you, to prosper you. He gave Himself for you in the life of His only Son. As that Son said so well in John 10:10, "I came that they may have and enjoy life, and have it in abundance (to the full, till it overflows)." But He, the one most acquainted with the grief and ravages of life, also made a tremendous point in the first half of this verse: "The thief comes only in order to steal and kill and destroy."

The next time you hear the promises of Jeremiah 29, the promise that God Almighty does indeed have a plan, a future, and a hope for you, remember they were spoken during 70 years of captivity, when Israel was despondent and needed to know God had more for them. When they were under the thumb of Babylonian rule, God poured these famous verses of hope into their hearts.

Depression may hold you captive for a season. You, however, are a child of the Living God. His Words of life never change.

~

I have been to the bottom and I found it was rock solid.

JOHN BUNYAN

The Pilgrim's Progress

I am weary with my groaning;

All night I soak my pillow with tears,

I drench my couch with my weeping.

My eye grows dim because of grief.

~

FROM PSALM 6

5

THE CRY
OF THE WOUNDED

During my years as a single mother, in an attempt to fit in with my pet-owning suburbanite neighbors, I decided to buy two Persian cats. Along with the two cats, I bought two bunnies. So for a time, the kids and I owned two very laid-back long-haired cats named Liam and Nick, and two extremely high-maintenance bunnies, Romeo and Juliet. The bunnies were banished to live outside our home when they began chewing away at the wallpaper and furniture. And their days were numbered when I found they had begun to spawn the entire city of Verona.

The cats, however, true to their breed, were just happy to be with the children and me—to step onto our work, climb over us, lounge around, and wait for whatever happened next. Courtney laid claim to Liam as hers, and Graham adored Nick (who was all white, named after the Jolly Ol' Saint.)

As it happened one cold December day, I was at the dentist's office, the chair back, ready to have my teeth cleaned, when I got an emergency phone call from home. Nicky had disappeared earlier, and Graham, ten years old at the time, was calling to tell me he'd located him.

"Mom! Mom! Nicky is crying, he's crying for us! He's crying—I can hear him!"

I bolted out of the chair. "Where is he, Graham?"

"I don't know, but I can hear him crying—believe me, Mom, it's Nicky!"

I had searched in vain for Nick all day and left out his favorite food to entice him back into the garage. Scouring the neighborhood from the car, calling out to the lovely, space-cadet cat and assuming he was lost, we prayed he would somehow find his way home.

"Mom! Come home! *Now!* He's trapped somewhere!—I can hear him calling me!"

"I've got to go home," I pleaded with the dental assistant, who was, thankfully, full of humor and more than familiar with our family. She smiled as I rushed out the office door.

At home, Graham met me with tears filling his big blue eyes, jumping around and demanding I go to the garage.

"He's in the garage, Mom! Listen!"

Sure enough, after stepping over the piles of junk I had stacked in front of the wall between the garage and the house, I heard a faint "meow…"

"See, see, see! You didn't believe me, but I *knew* he was there!"Graham was absolutely defiant.

I had to admit I couldn't believe it when I found one small hole in the wall and reached my arm as far in as I possibly could to discover a fury, shaking little Nick. He had made his way in and didn't have the good sense or the energy to follow the light back out to freedom.

My son's joy brought tears to my eyes as well.

We loved on Nicky, fed him, cleaned him up, and brought him back into the warm house.

He was crying for help and Graham heard him through the walls…

⟿

Depressed individuals are somewhat like dear little Nicky. They—we—find ourselves caught in between life and death—between wanting to live and wanting to die—between holding on and letting go—and our cries need to be heard. We build up walls of isolation, despair, crazy thinking, distorted images of ourselves. Walls keep us trapped. A weak spot in the armor, a slip from the ladder of life, a sudden loss, and we back or retreat into a place of hopeless darkness. Still we call out, most of us, in odd, strange ways for someone to hear, for someone to find us and pull us back into life again. Depression leaves the sufferer unable to help themselves.

What are some common symptoms of depression?

Changes in sleep behavior. A depressed person may find himself or herself either sleeping too much, not wanting to get out of bed, always tired; or unable to sleep, mind racing, waking and then experiencing the inability to go back to sleep. Sleep deprivation does strange things to people. It's commonly used on prisoners by their captors to break down their defenses. Imagine what disruption of sleep can do to the mental and physical health of the body.

Lack of interest in life and in what usually brings you joy. If you find yourself in a state of apathy, not caring much for anything that might normally engage your interest and even get your energy going, you are having more than just a "blue day." A persistent desire to keep your distance from people you love or activities that are uniquely your own raises a red flag for possible depression.

Changes in eating patterns. A danger sign for me that a depressive episode may be beginning is a loss of appetite. I lost almost ten pounds over 12 days in my first nosedive into clinical depression. If this sounds appealing to you, trust me, it's not the diet you're looking for. Severe weight loss is as damaging as severe weight gain. (Two surgeries for two precancerous places in my body accompanied the stress and weight loss.) Depression can take away the joy of eating and the desire to eat—or just the opposite may occur. Food may become the easiest place of comfort. When you're medicating yourself with food, self-image issues worsen with weight gain. This becomes another cycle of despair. Any eating patterns out of balance can be a sign of depression.

And anorexia and bulimia are both forms of depression! These eating disorders involve starving the body by eating the most minimal portions of food, or by eating and then inducing food loss by vomiting and laxatives. I don't know that many of us would see these compulsions having roots in depression, but this disorder is rising among depressed teenage women and middle-aged women, all of whom are trying to have some control over their otherwise out-of-control world. It's a cry for help when anyone you love, yourself first and foremost, begins to habitually practice unhealthy eating habits.

A stream of physical ailments. Depression, by its very nature of tearing apart eating and sleeping habits, combined with a lack of joy in life, can greatly break down the immune system. If you have an increased amount of physical problems, both real and imagined, such as tiredness, weakness, dizziness, headaches (migraine in particular), tightening of the chest, and breathing difficulties, please consult a doctor and ask the hard questions about depression. (For example, when I am depressed, my breathing patterns are very erratic. I will find myself holding my breath, very tense. At night I may wake from sleep with my body held tightly, not breathing. I have learned to practice simple breathing exercises to calm my system back into normalcy.)

Physical-intimacy issues. If you are depressed and are married, depression will most likely, for a time, wreck intimacy with your mate. Here again, some depressed people become demanding of sex, using this as a place to hide and medicate their pain. For most, though, sexual needs and other basic human needs are numbed out and no longer bring any satisfaction. Many depressed people have little or no desire for sexual intimacy, and they do not respond to physical touch. Because depression's tentacles reach into every aspect of one's being, a depressed person feels unattractive, worthless, and apathetic about life in general. Moms may have little energy for their children or spouse. Men may retreat into inactivity and lethargy.

The sad truth of it is that depressed ones feel so bad about themselves that they have no reserves to draw on for others, even the ones they care deeply for. The affection is buried under the disease. (The greatest commandment given to us by Jesus is to love God with all of our heart, mind, and soul, and then love our neighbor as ourself. This requires seeing ourself as God sees us.) And a person in the throes of depression has to relearn, remember, and re-embrace the love of God for themselves.

Tears, free-flowing weeping. Most people who suffer from depression cannot seem to control their tears. The faucet is turned on and appears to have tapped into the losses of the universe. Some call it "having the weeps." For me, it is the inability to manage my emotions. For everyone, it can be extremely embarrassing and frustrating. Tears tell us a lot about who we are.

> Whenever you find tears in your eyes, especially unexpected tears, it is well to pay closest attention. They are not only telling you something about the secret of who you are, but more often than not God is speaking to you through the mystery…of where, if your soul is to be saved, you should go next.[1]

God uses tears to alert our hearts and the hearts of those around us where we are on the roller coaster of life.

Perhaps God is using the depressed person's tears as a cry for mercy. Tears are not to be ignored. What makes us cry? If it is a state of hopelessness and despair, depression may be the root cause. But I believe in a God who understands tears caused by a broken spirit. "Jesus gives God a face, and that face is streaked with tears," Philip Yancey observes. Jesus understands pain and despair, and the cruelty of a world in need of hope. His isn't a pie-in-the-sky hope. It's real and relevant. In later chapters I'll look at just how the nuts and bolts of Christ-hope can be used in practical and spiritual terms.

A cloak of hopeless sadness. Depression colors life with gray and with black; it blocks out the light. Sufferers have no air of joy, no sense of purpose. They may try to mask their pain, even with manic activity (especially if they deal with bipolar issues.) Be on guard for these walking wounded, especially those in your family and your closest circle of friends. For those of us who deal with depression, we must take our emotional temperature: Does others' happiness stir in us feelings of resentment? Are our emotions brittle? Is unexplained anger coming out of us, shooting off in one direction or another?

Depression...anger...hopelessness...perpetual sadness: These are not the cross Christ asked any of us to bear. Yet the church at times has a tendency to view as holy martyrdom being resigned to a living life with ongoing, deep depression. "I began to seriously question my faith when I was suffering my second year of depression," writes author John Eldredge in his book *Waking the Dead.* "People in church saw my depressed face, and they complimented me on how I was such a good Christian. I thought the best way for a person to live is to keep his desires at a minimum so that he will be prepared to serve God."[2]

But a passionless life is a wasted life.

Christ died to renew our passion, not to remove it.

I can personally vouch for this: Depression cripples my ability to serve in the kingdom of God. However, when my illness is under control and I'm back climbing the ladder again, I can reach out to others and help them along. But merely existing is defeat.

Worry, anxiety, anger, irritability. You cannot be a human being without experiencing some of these emotions. It's when your life is *controlled* by these feelings that depression takes over. Almost all depression I've experienced and studied about has an element of anger involved, and for many it has been described as anger turned in on themselves. Anger can be the fertile ground for extreme worry about all aspects of life, anxiety over lost dreams, hostility and irritability at dashed expectations. When anger tips in a toxic direction, depression spreads like a rash through our hearts.

⤺

These are a number of easily identifiable warning signs of depression. They are by no means exhaustive. But a majority of these particular signs are present across the board in any stage of depression.

Listen to your life, your heart, your tears, your rage, your lack of rage, lack of tears, lack of sleep, lack of desire…Listen to the signs God has put into you and every precious creation of His, the physical and emotional alarms that go off when we need help.

We have a God who is passionately interested in every season of your life.

He wants anyone hurting to find rest and help and strength in Him. Depression offers us a chance to find His power when we have none of our own to draw from. The gig is up. The farce that any one of us can do this "life"-thing apart from God is thrown back in our face. We fall apart…and come apart in His hands. It seems we've lost so much ground and fallen so short of what we wanted our lives to be.

Yet, with God, time is not *going*—it is always coming, coming, coming, bringing new life, new hope, a new future, and the purest of healing.

On God's watch, nothing is wasted.

Breaking 400 years of silence between the writings of the Old and the New Testaments, the words spoken to man by an angel of God are never more applicable than to those who may despair: "Don't be afraid. God has heard your prayer."[3]

I thank God for my handicaps,

for through them, I have found myself,

my work, and my God.

~

HELEN KELLER
Gift of Darkness

6

SHADES OF BLACK

We have to know what we are fighting to win the war. This is all about taking the power out of depression, understanding what you are facing, and then moving on up your ladder with knowledge and healing. So don't give up on me here.

Listed below are some of the most common varieties of depression. Remember, you are not alone. I'm a card-carrying member of clinical depression (the genetic, not generic, brand!). Consider the following shades of this disease to see if anything rings true to your experience, or of someone you love.

Major Depression

Melancholia, clinical depression—this category seems to be the most widespread form of depression. Usually the person suffering recognizes that something is terribly wrong, but has been blindsided by the disease. Such a person shows many if not all of the symptoms previously mentioned. Left untreated, this type of depression can lead to a psychotic state or even suicide.

Most major depression is triggered by a sense of loss, coupled with a season of intense doubt and lack of purpose. One last disappointment, the straw that breaks the emotional backbone, is all it takes. For many this occurs in midlife, where a person may relate to the words of Solomon: "All is vanity!" If we have put all our hopes and dreams into a world system that has failed us, if we've put all our trust into a marriage, job, wealth, possessions, or position of status, and then "A" + "B" does not equal our personal view of "C," depression may take root. Conversely, the highly successful person may also find that once having achieved all expectations, there is still an empty hole in their soul. Each one is suffering loss.

For example, in the movie *About Schmidt,* we find a man in his mid-60s—retired, a widower, looking around his life with tearful confessions that he feels he has done nothing to give back to the world, left no mark of any significance. At the end of the film, Schmidt receives a simple letter from a young child. It confirms a life-changing impact he has made on one person. Schmidt weeps in heart-wrenching relief that indeed all was not vanity.

Clinical depression falls into this category of loss of purpose, loss of self, loss of dreams. The word *clinical* refers to a chemical imbalance in the brain, brought on by either genetic predispositions triggered by loss, or by genetic causes in and of themselves.

During my clinical depression, I discovered that on my mother's side of our family there is a history of many women who suffered chemical, genetic depression. My great-aunt Helen called and wrote to me often during my recovery to encourage me that the path I had chosen to climb my ladder again was a good one. She allowed me the space to fall apart, and then come together again, without shame. Aunt Helen helped me understand my predisposition to depression and the role it played in my bloodline. Losses of my marriage, relationships, and ministry, and a sense of failure, fed neatly into my DNA. Clinical depression would most likely have occurred on some level for me eventually, but it was propelled into my life by a season of many losses.

Referring to chemical, genetic imbalances, I want to help you understand what this means in the easiest terms possible. The brain has chemicals, called neurotransmitters, that operate as messengers between nerve cells. There are many types of these transmitters. One is called *monoamine.* There are three "messengers" in monoamine: *dopamine, noradrenaline,* and *serotonin.* These very important chemical ingredients control brain functions affecting appetite, sleep, and motivation. They are especially critical for emotional health. Think of these big words as mood messengers.

During depression, our mood messengers are confused, not working properly, depleted, out of synch, or perhaps not speaking to each other.

Take a deep breath and let's move on.

Other Types of Depression

Bipolar disorders. This condition seems to be on the rise in our culture—or at least, more readily diagnosed. Bipolar individuals tend to be highly charismatic, creative, and interesting, and will bounce from extreme highs to extreme lows with little middle ground between. The disorder can be effectively treated with medication and therapy, but the greatest risk to such a person is that they will gleefully go off their medication when on a high and then plunge into a low, thus creating a cycle of chaos in their lives. The manic period (the high side), untreated, lasts for an average of six months, followed by a sharp low lasting from eight to ten months. The death rate, due largely to accidental, risky behavior during the manic phase, is at around 15 percent for those who remain untreated. A high degree of accountability about the reality of their condition is a key element to maintaining balance with this form of depression.

Major depressive episodes with psychotic features. This shade of black usually stems from some sort of biological/genetic predisposition. The person's outward appearance will not mask the depression but will scream out that they are hurting, full of extreme anxiety, and not coping well. In some cases they falsely assume that others are "out to get them," and in extreme cases, they hear voices.*

Schizophrenia. This horrible shade of black is characterized primarily by a thought disorder and secondarily by a mood disorder. One source notes his experience of it was as if "someone took his brain and shattered it on concrete." It is the most heartbreaking and difficult of depressive conditions to treat. Please do not despair if you are, or if you have a loved one battling schizophrenia, for many revolutionary medications and methods are being discovered every year. But watch for the symptoms: autism, hearing voices, hallucinations, delusions, being overexcited and out of touch with reality, exhibiting violent displays of anger and unexplained outbursts of despair.

Seasonal affective disorder (SAD). Recently I heard a beautiful young woman raise her hand and timidly ask for prayer in a Sunday morning service. "It sounds silly for me to ask this when there are so many other serious problems we need to pray for... but there are some of us who have a hard time now that the days are shorter and it gets dark so early. Will you pray for us too?" This is a fairly new category of depression, which includes those who are regularly depressed according to changes in the length of daylight. The person might sleep too much, feel weighed down, be unable to attend social events, crave carbohydrates in excess, become anxious and sad, all due to lack of enough sunlight.

A talented writer, wife, and mother of five describes her literal fight against darkness:

> For as far back as I can remember, I've suffered from Seasonal Affective Disorder. Exuberantly alive during the

---

* Hearing voices has been widely assumed in Christian circles to be a sign of satanic influence on the body and mind. Current studies indicate, however, that new medications pinpointing particular areas in the brain completely eliminate the voices and behavioral confusion in these patients. While research continues—and people of faith continue to rightly believe that we battle an enemy in both · spiritual and physical realms—I would still encourage all not to rush to judgment. Frequently, psychotic episodes, including hearing voices, are a chemical brain disorder—those mood messengers are on "stun."

spring and summer, I am a bundle of creative energy. In the fall and winter, I withdraw into myself to suffer from lethargy and a moodiness that has my whole family tip-toeing around me. As I grew older, the symptoms grew worse, until one winter it overwhelmed me. I couldn't sleep, I couldn't think, I couldn't stop crying. Instead of gaining weight as I usually did in the winter, I lost 20 pounds. I didn't realize my SAD had spiraled into a clinical depression.

My friend sought medical help, and she now has control of the seasonal onslaught. For her, medication was needed only until she and her doctor found other ways to treat the light deprivation. The good news is, there are phototherapy devices that can be used, and apparently the artificial replication of sunlight has a wonderful curative effect on a patient.

∽

I have not given an exhaustive list above. I am not a doctor, and I do not have the expertise to speak to every form of the disease. However, I can relate to the experience of major clinical-depressive episodes, and over time, I've researched enough to be able to address depression and recovery from an overall—and highly personal—perspective.

∽

Let me be the one to say to you,
"You will *not* always feel this way."

∽

The above types are the most commonly diagnosed forms of depression; many other minor categories fall under the headings.

Depression, being a disorder of the emotions, a disruption of the juices in a person's unique chemical makeup, makes it an ever-changing disease. However, the shafts of light breaking through in the treatment of these disorders have never before been so bright. The spiritual, medical, and physical treatments available in our century are at last battling back the darkness from every side.

I encourage you to keep reading as we explore exciting aspects of recovery and relief. Let me write that word again—relief! How I longed for relief in my darkest days and ached for someone to tell me I wouldn't always have to feel so very hopeless.

Let me be the one to say to you, "You will *not* always feel this way."

You can get better.

You can get well.

Don't minimize your pain, but with understanding and trust in God, move ahead one step at a time into wholeness again.

Denial is put to death by knowledge. Knowledge puts to death the mystery of the disease. Hope is the key to finding help, holding onto God's love, and knowing in Him there is a way out of the darkness.

> A Scottish preacher...lost his wife suddenly and after her death admitted in a sermon that he did not understand this life of ours. But still less could he understand how people facing loss could abandon faith. "You people in the sunshine may believe the faith, but we in the shadow *must* believe it. We have nothing else." [1]

Whether you are one who believes in God and His love, or just someone reaching out from your pain to search for help, I know that God wants you healthy and well again. He will meet you right where you are and move with you through the valley of the shadow into light again. He's a gentleman. He'll never ask you to thank Him. I pray you will, however, find your knees bowing as you recover, not in despair but in gratitude for a Father God who weeps with those who weep, who suffered through giving His Son to defeat hopelessness, and who loves us unconditionally no matter where He finds us on our ladder of life.

You're in Good Company

Who gets depressed?

We all have a down day here and there. The blues come and go. But who gets seriously, clinically, medically incapacitated by depression?

You may be surprised.

Putting to rest the argument that only the weak of heart heel to the feet of depression, let's take a look at some biblical figures whose bouts with depression were not omitted from God's Word. Stories of depression chronicled in the Bible give us a place of comfort and camaraderie with some of our depressed forefathers. God's love through His word doesn't hide from the human condition. Our radical God is perpetually, personally involved in the process of redeeming and restoring our loss.

Naomi. Perhaps in reading the beautiful story of Ruth, we skip too quickly over the heartache and suicidal words of Ruth's mother-in-law. Naomi lost so much—her husband, both of her sons—and she begged her daughters-in-law to leave her to die:

> Call me not Naomi [pleasant]; call me Mara [bitter], for the Almighty has dealt very bitterly with me. I went out full, but the Lord has brought me home again empty. Why call me Naomi, since the Lord has testified against me, and the Almighty has afflicted me?[2]

King Solomon. The wisest, most powerful, and wealthiest of all men who ever lived wrote these words in Eccelesiates—his view on the suffering world before him:

> I saw all the people who were mistreated here on earth. I saw their tears and that they had no one to

comfort them. Cruel people had all the power, and there was no one to comfort those they hurt. I decided that the dead are better off than the living.[3]

Jonah. Consider one of the rather humorous bouts of depression recorded in the Bible, that of the prophet Jonah. It's a short book with a huge tale to tell about being a person of faith, angry with God for actually staying true to His character.

Jonah was commissioned to take a message of redemption to the enemies of Israel in Nineveh. En route, the reluctant prophet managed to have himself thrown off of the ship he traveled on during a storm. Maybe this was his first attempt at ending his life.

Jonah had gone in the opposite direction from where God had sent him and ended up in a mess of trouble. This prophet who had intimate conversations with God was in such despair that he lived through three days and nights in the belly of a whale before being spit up on dry land. While in the guts of the giant fish he spoke of God's deliverance: "When I was in danger, I called to the Lord, and he answered me. I was about to die, so I cried to you, and you heard my voice."[4]

Stepping onto dry ground, he took God's commandment of repentance and redemption to the people of Nineveh. It's fairly clear Jonah had little faith in his enemies' desire for a change of heart. They did the unthinkable, though, and took God at His word.

Upon seeing his enemies restored to God, Jonah was overwhelmed with outrage and depression. When the mercy of God won the day, Jonah was so depressed he demanded God to put him to death. In anger he cried out to the Lord,

> When I was still in my own country this is what I said would happen, and that is why I quickly ran away to Tarshish. I knew that you are a God who is kind and shows mercy. You don't become angry quickly, and

you have great love. I knew you would choose not to cause harm. So now I ask you, Lord, please kill me. It is better for me to die than to live.[5]

Interesting response of Mr. Jonah—what to do when God's mercy transforms even the darkest of hearts. The elder brother of the prodigal son didn't know what to do with the party his father threw for the wild-child younger son who came home full of godly sorrow and repentance. I also recall Max Lucado's honesty in wrestling with what to do with the conversion of the mass murder Jeffrey Dahmer before Dahmer was killed in prison. What do we do with forgiveness, a critical issue for the depressed? (We'll look more at this in chapter 10.)

Job. Surely the poster child for loss, Job lost his entire family, children, property, and health all in a matter of days, stammered forth the pain of all who suffer the blackness of depression:

> I shout, "I have been wronged!" But I get no answer.
> I scream for help but I get no justice.
> God has blocked my way so I cannot pass;
> He has covered my paths with darkness.
> He beats me on every side until I am gone,
> He destroys my hope like a fallen tree.[6]

Hannah. The story of Hannah usually brings a smile and an inner "ahh…isn't God good?" when we remember this mother longing for a child and finally giving birth to Samuel. But before she experienced motherhood, Hannah endured what I believe to be years of major depression. Living with another wife, Penninah, who gave birth over and over again, who flaunted her children before a barren Hannah, resulted in a condition that reflects depressive symptoms.

By the time Hannah was discovered by Eli the priest, she was unable to eat and unable to stop crying. Her husband had asked her why she was "so sad" and could not stop crying. Eli believed her to be drunk because only her lips moved as she sat crying out to God in despair. Hannah said to the priest, "No, sir, I have not drunk any wine or beer. I am a deeply troubled woman, and I was telling the Lord about all my problems. Don't think I am an evil woman. I have been praying because I have many troubles and am very sad."[7]

Jesus. For me, the most compelling words about depression come from the mouth of Jesus. In the garden of Gethsemane before His betrayal and crucifixion, He sweat great drops of blood. This is a medical condition caused from extreme physical and mental stress. He then cried out the very human, agonized words, "My heart is full of sorrow, to the point of death...Abba, Father! You can do all things. Take away this cup of suffering. But do what you want, not what I want."[8]

And from the cross where Christ hung came the echo of the words of David, most likely distilling into one sentence the primal sentiment of every heart filled with black depression: "My God, my God, why have you rejected me?"[9]

More Recent Figures

Others throughout history have suffered bouts of debilitating depression. The great Winston Churchill spoke of depression as the "black dog"—a poignant metaphor of an all-too-familiar animal that curls up next to one's feet at night like clockwork. Consider Abraham Lincoln. So burdened was he with his call in life, he once said, "I am now the most miserable man living. To remain as I am is impossible. I must die or be better." His wife, Mary Todd Lincoln, we now understand, endured spells of intense depression and migraines and tragically died alone in her madness.

The poetess Emily Dickinson's words, often eloquent and poignantly painful, bring to the surface her battle with depression and, ironically, offer through the life of her poetry a richly empathetic voice. (See an example on page 26.) She, like too many others, took her life.

Untreated depression caused the suicide death of the despairing artist Vincent Van Gogh and darkened the heart of author Dorothy Parker. The words of esteemed author Ernest Hemingway—"Life breaks us all in unexpected ways, but some of us grow strong in the broken places"—comment sadly on the history of his work since he committed suicide. His words echo a truth beautifully written yet impossible for him to grasp during his manic–depressive episodes.

Honesty Today

For centuries, poets, doctors, authors, actors, and laymen of all walks of life who suffered depression had little help or hope. Many turned to alcohol for relief and white-knuckled their way through life as best they knew how.

Thankfully, several current high-profile individuls have made their struggles with depression known. Their brave honesty encourages others to reach out from the shame and fear that accompany this disease to find relief.

Athletes such as Terry Bradshaw and Ricky Williams have appeared on national television to describe their suffering with anxiety disorders and depression. With these admissions, depression loses more of its unmentionable reputation and becomes more readily identified as a treatable illness. Depression is being given credibility. This credibility, pushing away the fear that's surrounded the mythology of depression, will, I hope, save countless lives.

"Looking back," said Bradshaw, four-time Super Bowl winner, a member of the Football Hall of Fame, and two-time Emmy winner for Outstanding Sports Personality, "I have been depressed for most of my life, even when I was a teenager. Finally, having a name for what I was feeling—depression—explained a lot about my actions."

Ted Turner, once *Time* magazine's Man of the Year, revealed the ravages depression took on his family. His father took his own life before he reached the age of 55. Turner began to be obsessed with a fear he would not live longer than his dad. He would talk often of suicide, and acted out by tempting fate in reckless adventures that could have taken his life. His father had been a highly troubled man, who had beaten his son with hangers or a razor strap when he disappointed him. In 1985 Turner finally went to a psychiatrist for help and began his journey up the ladder of his life again. As *Time* magazine noted, "Turner is a classic example of the observation that achievement doesn't mean happiness; instead it's how we live rather than what we do that leads to peace."[10]

For people of faith, the same principle can be applied. We can't all be strong enough or good enough or well enough to avoid disease. Some have physical disease. For others, it comes in less tangible mental packages.

Shelia Walsh has written eloquently of her season of depression and her hospitalization. The angel-voiced speaker and author travels with the Women of Faith organization and gives voice for so many who need to know that depression strikes—and strikes hard—even at the women who love God most tenaciously.

Internationally known television journalist Jane Pauley has shown tremendous resolve in making public her discovery of her bipolar depression. When someone like Ms. Pauley says out loud that she was clueless about her mood swings and their effect on her life and family until she was diagnosed, you can almost hear a collective sigh of relief.

What Does Depression Feel, Taste, Sound Like?

You are not alone. Your loved one is not alone. Read and listen to the sound of suffering from just a few I've read from, met, and heard from.

I particularly remember the lamentable near disappearance of my voice. A friend observed later that it was the voice of a ninety-year-old. I found myself eating only for subsistence; food, like everything else within the scope of sensation, was utterly without savor. Most distressing of all the instinctual disruptions was that of sleep, along with the complete absence of dreams. Exhaustion combined with sleeplessness is a rare torture.

William Styron
Darkness Visible

I have no faith. Or, rather, I have faith but it doesn't seem to apply.

John Updike
A Month of Sundays

In my experience, the landscape ahead was shrouded with uncertainty. I couldn't see one day ahead of me. I became a foot watcher, walking through airports or the grocery store staring at my feet, methodically moving through a misty world. One foot, then the other. Even before that I came to associate faith with simply tying my shoes. Some days, especially early on, it was the only act of faith I could muster.

Billy Sprague
Letter to a Grieving Heart

The air seems thick and resistant, as though it were full of mushed-up bread. Becoming depressed is like going blind, the darkness at first gradual, then encompassing; it is like going deaf, hearing less and less until a terrible silence is all around you, until you cannot make any sound of your own to penetrate the quiet. It is like feeling your clothing slowly turning into wood on your body, a stiffness in the elbows and the knees progressing to a terrible weight and an isolating immobility that will atrophy you and in time destroy you.

Andrew Solomon
Noonday Demon

I guess I've been disappointed enough times that I simply pray for less and less in order not to be disappointed over and over.

Anonymous voice from Iowa

I only take baths now because the water beating down on me from the shower is too much to deal with in the morning and seems, these days, like a violent way to begin the day. Driving seems like such an effort. So does visiting the ATM, shopping—you name it.

Laura
as quoted by Andrew Solomon, *Noonday Demon*

She knew that death was only a door to the kingdom where Jesus would welcome her, there would be no more crying there, no suffering, but meanwhile she was fat, her heart hurt, and she lived alone with her ill-tempered little dogs, tottering around her dark little house full of Chinese figurines and old *Sunday Tribunes*.

Garrison Keillor
"Faith of Old Aunt Marie"

I cannot explain my depression to anyone. It is nonrational, and flies in the face of my comfortable life. It colors my outlook on the entire world and I harbor it as a secret point of view that no one else shares or can enter into. Nothing seems more real to me, when I am depressed. The darkness defines my life.

Anonymous
as quoted by Philip Yancey, *Disappointment with God*

Christ has cleaned up bigger messes than mine, and I know that. Right now, however, I don't "feel" any hope, and I am weary and exhausted, tired of fighting and hanging on. It's been years now. First my illness, then my wife's, then my family and now my marriage. The other day I sat on the couch and wept and cried to the Lord, "God, I cannot take this anymore. I cannot take it!" I'm not sure what I expected to happen; perhaps I expected a lightning bolt of peace to shoot through my body or for my wife to walk into the house yelling, "I adore you!" How I longed for some sort of epiphany or new infilling...anything...

A dear friend's e-mail

The One Who Weeps with Us

Before I faced clinical depression, I thought only weaklings, only the real screwups in life were ever depressed. It was a strange, far-off disorder I didn't want to know anything about. It was scary, and if I met someone who was depressed I wanted to back away, fearful that their mood might "rub off" on me. Then, as with divorce and single parenthood, I found myself in another unthinkable land—this time, the land of clinical depression—one more "this can't happen to me."

It's terribly difficult to comprehend the horrors of this disease. Certainly, if you are living with someone who has any form of depression, you are suffering right along with them. You may want to shake them hard, or shout (as a dear friend called it, "The

First Phrase in the Top-Ten Worst Things to Say to a Depressed Person"), "Snap out of it!"

Believe me, when you are in a major depression there is nothing you long for more than the ability to snap out of it... shake it off...get over it...have enough faith...enough something...enough anything to climb out of the pit. But God knows it's never that simple.

Yes, I think He does understand.

Wth all due reverence, I would like to suggest that God Himself, in some unknowable way, is acutely acquainted with pain, heartache, and even depression. Throughout the written Word we find God hurting so much that He reaches from heaven to earth to bring hope to His garden filled with hurting fallen ones.

In Genesis, God's pain is clear in the words spoken of Him before the waters of the flood fell: "The Lord regretted that He had made man on earth, and He was grieved at heart."[11] Still, there was Noah and his family and the amazing animals left to save.

God was again moved to pity when Abraham asked Him to spare the people of Sodom and Gomorrah from fiery destruction. "What if there are 50 people who love you Lord? What if there are 40, 30, 20....just 10?"

In the book of Jeremiah, God moaned to his prophet as if He were in a state of shock at the condition of His people: "Inquire among the nations: Who has ever heard anything like this? A most horrible thing has been done by Virgin Israel...My people have forgotten me."[12] In these words I hear the shuddering broken heart of an Almighty Creator!

Abraham Heschel pondered this scripture and wondered over the wounded heart of God:

> The melancholy heart of God's words...God is mourning Himself. With Israel's distress came the affliction of God, His displacement, His homelessness in the land, in the world...for Israel's desertion was not merely an injury to man; it was an insult to God.

This was the voice of God who felt shunned, pained and offended.[13]

Yet God's great pain is always overcome by His great mercy.

From the Son of God, hear a cry for healing from the cross, "Father, forgive them, for they know not what they do."

As we take depression to the cross, I know we will find a merciful God, weeping and walking the floor with us, holding our faces in His hands to catch our tears. The book of Revelation tells of the golden bowls that hold the prayers of the saints.[14] Our Father treasures the prayers poured out by His beloved. We are not forgotten.

In case you feel as I once did, that God was a bit too busy to notice I was sinking in the quicksand of depression, read this promise from your passionate, ever-faithful Father:

> Can a woman forget the baby she nurses?
> Can she feel no kindness for the child to which she
>   gave birth?
> Even if she could forget her children, I will not forget
>   you.
> See, I have written your name on my hand.
> Anyone who trusts in me will not be disappointed.[15]

The absence of God in the world
and about the storm of his absence,
both without and within,
because it is unendurable, unliveable,
drives us to look to the eye of the storm.

~

FREDERICK BUECHNER

7

HOPE IN THE
EYE OF THE STORM

My friend, whether or not you feel it (and feelings are not what define who you are and where you are going), you have already begun your steps back into recovery. You have now stepped up the ladder with some understanding and knowledge of what you are fighting, and the symptoms of this disease. You also have under you the steps of fellow friends of faith and others who have gone before and are climbing with you.

The next major step back up the ladder into living again is to find your spiritual footing. I hope you will work under the assumption, whether or not it appears to be "working," that God is in the darkness beside you, whispering into your soul words of comfort, not condemnation. He is the cornerstone, not the one cornering you.

Prayer and spiritual healing are absolutely essential to depression recovery.

"Is the death of my prayer the end of my intimacy with God, or the beginning of a new communion, beyond words, emotions and bodily sensation?"[1]

The inability to pray is not the end of your relationship with God. It's a by-product of the depression. God hears every sigh, every whisper, and catches every tear.

Even those who do not operate from a religious worldview see a strong correlation between depression recovery and a need for faith:

> Another system has helped many people to cope with their illness, and that is faith. Human consciousness may be seen bound by the sides of a triangle: the theological, the psychological, and the biological. Religious belief is one of the primary ways that people accommodate depression. Religion provides answers to unanswerable questions. It can help people survive depressive episodes. It gives reasons to live. It grants us dignity and purpose in our helplessness. Faith is a great gift. Faith in its essence offers hope.[2]

The Church—A Place of Hope?

A kernel of hope, a sliver of hope, any form of hope is essential in depression recovery. Without hope, yes, people do perish.

The church at large must become more and more a source of comfort, and drop its fear about depression. Hope waits to come alive again within its doors.

Divorce was the "unforgivable sin" for quite a long while. Finally, the church was forced by sheer numbers of its own family and clergy to admit that divorced people were starving for mercy and healing. Slowly programs began for divorced, single-again members and their children.

Other issues like pornography, homosexuality, and now depression will require the leaders of our churches to open their hearts and ears to be the arms, feet, hands, and voice of Jesus to an aching world. This is not a call for selling out, rewriting Scripture, or bowing to the idol of political correctness. It is, however, a challenge for the church to become equipped with counselors, prayer warriors, and godly, grace-drenched teaching.

One of my dearest friends, Luci Freed, worked for years as the director of what is now called The Hope Clinic, where alternative choices are offered to women considering abortion. Luci presently has a private practice as a clinical psychologist. She has an understanding of the shame and the stigma that depression hangs around our neck like a neon sign for those of us who deal with the disease.

Time I spend with Luci usually comes around to a conversation about depression and a mutual, resounding, "if only!" declaration of frustration over how the church deals with depressed individuals. Mostly, churches don't deal at all. It's too weird to talk about depression. Depressed people must be really wrong with God. Depression is maybe...kind of...sort of...in the category with demon possession or witchcraft, right?

Wrong.

The myths must be put to rest.

Far too many people sitting in church every week are going home to dark houses, filled with hours of desperation and fear and thoughts of suicide. There are many ways to retreat from life.

"Someone told me years ago that a church is at its best when it is a cross between a hospital and a bar!" Luci once said. "The very spiritual who would never think of entering a bar look at me with shock when I say this. Maybe I should say that the bar might even be a more attractive choice if the hospital was staffed by uneducated and unsympathetic caregivers. The analogy here is not about a drinking, carousing atmosphere but a place of acceptance. The popular television series *Cheers* was enticing because 'everybody knows your name,' and they were 'always glad when you came.' How much our churches need this kind of welcoming aura for the hurting, depressed ones among us."

Luci told me about a friend who suffered silently from years of depression until one day she asked her the question, "If I attended your church and sat on the back row for months, crying through the entire service, would I be welcomed, loved, or accepted as I am?"

There's a story about a public sinner who was excommunicated and forbidden to enter his church.

> He took his woes to God. "They won't let me in, Lord, because I am a sinner."
>
> "What are you complaining about?" said God. "They won't let Me in either."[3]

A Place for Honesty?

After I spoke at a women's conference, a woman sidled up to me and whispered, "You know, if we all opened our purses and dumped out the contents, I think there would be a lot more said about depression around here."

The church does a terrific job of holding up the physically ill.

> There is no magic cure for a person in pain. Mainly, such a person needs love, for love instinctively detects what is needed.

Yet when it comes to a mental illness, the stained-glass doors quietly close and lock.

I met a man who went through a dark depression after the birth of his child with Down syndrome. At church, he found the same platitudes that greet many people of faith in the grips of depression.

"Why isn't the good news of Jesus good enough for you?"

"Pray more...you'll be fine...just pray more."

"God must have a reason...you have to accept life!"

Shame-filled thoughts torment a depressed person of faith.

Empty admonitions like the above run like a badly scratched recording through their thoughts. Guilt flows freely. No one I know has ever been shamed into mental or physical health.

What would God have us do?

What would Jesus say?

I like how Philip Yancey addresses pain: "In short, there is no magic cure for a person in pain. Mainly, such a person needs love, for love instinctively detects what is needed."[4]

What we do know, by watching Christ's words and the path of His feet, is that He did not condemn, but rather spoke hope to the hopeless. His harshest words were saved for the pious religious leaders of the day, whom He charged with demanding the impossible from people under their leadership, so as to break their backs with a load of guilt.

A Place for the Brokenhearted

From those acutely aware of their broken state, the Bible records—without softening—shouts of pain.

> How long will you forget me, Lord?
> Forever?
> How long will you hide from me?
> How long must I worry and feel sad in my heart all day?
> How long will my enemy win over me?
> Lord, look at me.
> Answer me, my God;
> Tell me, or I will die.[5]

God's merciful answer is found in my favorite passage:

> The Lord is close to the brokenhearted
> And he saves those whose spirits have been crushed.[6]

God draws near to the weak spirit, the down-and-out soul, the person who feels that the "Too Late—So Give Up" notice has arrived in the mail. As people who follow God, are we not to do the same?

The One Who Will Take You Through

My pastor and friend, Scotty Smith, is a wise man of God. He's seen his share of tear-stained faces show up at his door. I thank the Lord that Scotty didn't shame me for my broken spirit. He handled me with care, and with methodical guidance. I desperately needed someone I respected to accept me and to represent hope I couldn't find in myself.

Now I am in a position of doing what Scotty did for me. I can speak hope to you. And it's not a sloppy promise. If it were only from me, I'd put no stock in it. What I offer you is my empathy as one who has been through the dark nights of depression. My hope lies in my faith that God will see me through anything, if I keep Him in the center of my heart.

This promise is one I put on a sticky note where I could see it every morning: "I...will instruct you and teach you in the way you should go; I will counsel you with My eye upon you."[7] With God in charge of the center of my heart, I trusted Him with each choice—from counseling to medications, work choices, and even how to say "no."

I cannot give you a neat, simple guide to the mending of your soul. That's up to God, and it's between you and Him. Maybe the best hope I can give is to say, "I've been where you are, and I'm still here! It's going to get better! You are going to make it!"

And I can point you to the promised hope of a God whose words never fail:

> I have called you by your name; you are Mine.
> When you pass through the waters, I will be with you, and through the rivers, they will not overwhelm you. When you walk through the fire, you will not be burned or scorched, nor will the flame kindle upon you...
> Fear not, for I am with you...
> Do not [earnestly] remember the former things; neither consider the things of old. Behold, I am doing

a new thing! Now it springs forth…I will even make
a way in the wilderness and rivers in the desert.[8]

Can you count the number of times "through" is used here?
Three times! Through the heartbreak, through the darkness,
through the fires…God *will* be there.

As your spirit begins to heal, beloved, take verses from God's
word and write them down and put them where you'll see them.
Make a bracelet for your wrist…put a note on your computer at
school or work…across the mirror in your bathroom at home…
let your mind be immersed in God's light and push back the dark.

⤴

Along with using all manner of Post-it notes, please consider
the following suggestions:

***Find a circle of close friends or family you can ask to pray for
you,*** in the same way the paralyzed man was lowered to Jesus by
his friends for healing. Unable to pray himself, this man's friends
gave him to the Lord. You need to admit you are depressed to
ones you can trust. Ask them to stand in a place of hope for you,
to be your own personal stretcher-bearers.

Fall apart in God's arms. When I was depressed I had little
energy for prayer and little belief that it would matter. It helped
me to know that others were able to believe what I could not. And
placing my wounded heart into the palms of God's hands, the
hands that had formed me, gave me a sense of security. I read
everything I could find on depression recovery. (There are sources
listed in the back of this book.) The Psalms are filled with expres-
sions of depression, and the words of David and other writers in
the Bible validated my experience. You may find you have little
physical energy. Reading doesn't take a lot. Find a place, a couch
or chair perhaps, somewhere you feel you can stack a pile of

books up around you and read, journal if you can, and drench
your mind in truth.

Talk openly to God. Tell Him everything—the works—hold
nothing back, especially feelings of loss, anger, and frustration.
Be real with God. Get in the boxing match and duke it out. His
shoulders are big enough, and He already knows the pain you are
feeling, the shame or guilt or unresolved areas in your life. Get it
out in the open. It's good for your soul to begin to rid yourself of
any toxic spiritual junk that may be backed up inside you.

Begin to find the center of yourself again—the core of your
being and purpose for living. My medical doctor believes all
depression recovery begins with finding the "center of our circle"
again, and with a central focus on worshiping God. During
depression, worship of God can perhaps best be viewed as your
efforts to get well in His hands. A life lived fully is in and of itself
a tremendous act of worship.

Imagine that you are the center of a circle. In that circle with
you is your connection with God. This intimacy with God is critical to how you see yourself, view the world, make choices, and
face what life brings. The next circle around the center might be
a relationship with your spouse, then a circle representing your
children. Next is your vocation—then your friendships, family,
dreams, hobbies—the circles going out and around your center
like rings around a planet.

When a disconnection occurs in the very center of your heart
it affects everything else spilling out around you. Plainly put,
when you and God aren't tight, you will come unwound.

> If you want joy, power, peace, eternal life, you must
> get close to or even into the thing that has them. They
> are not a sort of prize which God could, if He chose,
> just hand out to anyone. They are a great fountain of
> energy and beauty spurting up at the very centre of
> reality. If you are close to it, the spray will wet you: if

you are not, you will remain dry. Once a man is united to God, how could he not live forever? Once a man is separated from God, what can he do but wither and die?[9]

As you reestablish your trust in God, or perhaps ask Him into the center of your circle for the first time, as you begin to pour out your deepest disappointments and ask for His healing, the center of your heart will begin to stabilize. Don't worry about being "fixed" to get right with God. Just grab onto His words, His love, with all you have.

Yoking the Heart

Jesus invites us to take his yoke, saying we will find it less burdensome than the ones we have taken upon ourselves. Taking on a yoke doesn't sound like a party. But in depression we row our boats down the river of denial until we hit an iceberg. My pastor quietly said to me, "Bonnie, I've watched you barrel through loss after loss and just keep going. At some point, I knew you would hit a wall." Depression was my wall. When depression threw me off course, I came face-to-face with the question of what I had yoked myself to.

All of us strap our hopes onto something, someone, some dream, some vision of how life will unfold. Yoking the heart to a whim. Yoking the heart to a flawed relationship, or to a person who can never fill what only God understands…Having personally tied my expectations to all manner of false gods, I admit it took depression to convince me that Jesus is trying to spare me pain by offering me a place beside Him, under His yoke. His invitation is steeped in delight:

> Come to Me, all you who labor and are heavy-laden and overburdened, and I will cause you to rest. [I will ease and relieve and refresh your souls.] Take My yoke upon you and learn of Me, for I am gentle (meek) and humble (lowly) in heart, and you will find rest (relief

and ease and refreshment and recreation and blessed quiet) for your souls. For My yoke is wholesome (useful, good—not harsh, hard, sharp or pressing, but comfortable, gracious, and pleasant), and My burden is light and easy to be borne.[10]

The yoke of Jesus has me under the covering of His arms. What a picture! I hear him saying, "Come and step inside this yoke with Me and be bonded to My strength, not your own. Become intertwined with My healing. I know how hard it is to be a human. I'm stronger, so when you are weak, I'll carry you. This yoke will never tear you down, wear you down, or give out. Let's walk one step at a time together."

Brennan Manning describes the power of God's magnificent love for us in our most unlovely moments:

Jesus comes not for the super-spiritual but for the wobbly and the weak-kneed who know they don't have it all together, and who are not too proud to accept the handout of amazin' grace. As we glance up, we are astonished to find the eyes of Jesus open with wonder, deep with understanding, and gentle with compassion.[11]

Be astonished—because it is outrageous to know we have a Savior who isn't put off by depression.

Be speechless—just close your eyes, and ask this wildly passionate lover of your soul to come into the center of your life.

Be courageous—begin to believe there is hope.

"O Israel, hope in the LORD," David says, "from this time forth and forever."

Hope like Israel. Hope for deliverance the way Israel hoped, and you are already half-delivered.

~

Hope beyond hope, and——like Israel in Egypt, in Babylon, in Dachau——you hope also beyond the bounds of your own captivity, which is what depression is.

FREDERICK BUECHNER

Whistling in the Dark

Christ Himself said that those

who are sick need a physician.

~

FRANK MINIRTH AND PAUL MEIER
Happiness Is a Choice

8

PERMISSION FOR PRESCRIPTIONS

Will somebody please just knock me out? All I want to do is shut my brain off and sleep!" I begged my doctor though tears. For almost two weeks, I'd slept in tiny spurts, one hour maybe, two maximum. The rest of the time my mind raced, I cried, I lost my appetite, and I began to have visions of going barking mad.

No wonder sleep deprivation is used to torture prisoners. Without proper sleep, the mind and body are highly vulnerable to all manner of delusional thinking. I became so desperate for sleep, I would have admitted to almost anything if my captor promised some rest. Instead, my captor—clinical depression— took me on a roller coaster ride. Up one hill I would barely be able to walk, dragging, weeping, body and soul sluggish. Then came the downward dive, and my mind would race, driven by anxiety, worry, pain, with sleep an impossibility.

What my doctor patiently put into simple terms was a defin- ition of the depression dance: My body was hungry and staying awake to be fed while my mind was racing, uninterested in food, and unable to rest. I was caught up in a downward plunge. By the time I was treated, hospitalization was suggested.

Amazing how primal a mother's instincts are. Even nearly out of my mind, I made an immediate decision to avoid being hospitalized. There were two children who needed a mom.

But Courtney and Graham needed a *healthy* mom.

When the doctor suggested medication, I had the knee-jerk reaction most people do: "Do I have to take medication?" And the voices of shame and guilt began rehearsing for a dark opera. "You are such a failure!" sang one little demon. "Oh ye of little faith, how far you've fallen," chimed in another.

I was at the end of myself.

Thankfully, the people who cared about me confirmed in louder tones that I needed to do whatever the doctor thought was best. When I filled three prescriptions and made my way home, I felt the first anticipation that perhaps I would at least get some rest.

However, my body was in such poor chemical condition that it took almost a solid year before I was strong again. And the journey through various medications until I found the ones that helped me was difficult, but necessary—and well worth the process.

The meds helped me get from a negative 50 back to an even 0.

From a more solid base, I began to climb back into life again.

It took medication to help me find the strength for counseling and more energy for healing prayer.

Operating from at least zero, I had a fighting chance to see the joy in my life and, as Emily Dickinson's poem encourages, to "dwell in possibility." (This quote hangs in my kitchen painted on a piece of ivory wood above the stove.) This truth comes from a writer who would have benefited from all the treatments now available to depressives. This lovely poet, who poignantly articulated the pain and joy of the human experience, lived in a time when there were no clear definitions or effective treatments for the extreme melancholia that colored her life. Drowning in pain, she had little energy to swim through the waters of depression, and eventually she took her own life.

A Question of Medication

> People who are depressed are in over their heads and don't know how to swim. They work very hard at living, at trying to solve their problems, but their efforts are unproductive because they lack the skills necessary to support themselves in deep water.[1]

Depression recovery may require medication when you are in over your head and drowning in the disease. Not everyone who suffers with depression needs medication. But I strongly urge that questions about medication be openly explored with a trusted physician.

Chemical, clinical imbalances in the brain—when those mood stabilizers are not communicating well—can be effectively treated and reconnected with simple antidepressants. The medical field has a variety of options, many of which might only be needed for a short period of time until the depression begins to lift and a patient regains their equilibrium.

This book is dedicated to my great-aunt Helen. She is the youngest of my grandmother's siblings, the youngest of ten children. I don't often get to visit this lovely, intelligent, godly woman, who lives with her husband in Arkansas. But she helped save me during the beginning of my depression; her voice was one that spoke spiritual hope to me and gave me permission for my prescriptions. No one in my family had mentioned the several women on my maternal side who had struggled with serious clinical depression. How I wish I had known about my predisposition to depression. Through gentle letters and phone calls from Aunt Helen, my personal history book was opened and a few skeletons came out of the closet.

"When I went through my depression, there were no medications available," Aunt Helen said bluntly. "The doctor gave me vitamin B-12 shots and sent me home to live with my mother for several months. Now you take that medicine, Bonnie, and thank God for it! It doesn't mean you aren't a good person, or that you don't love God...You don't need to carry any shame. Just get well."

My angel-aunt's declaration bathed me in absolution.

❧

The past decade of dealing with depression has been filled with lessons about the reality of the disease and my limitations. Depression brings with it one large dose of humility.

Several times I've decided to wean myself off the small amount of meds I take. Without consulting my doctor, I will cut back slowly over a few weeks—and then hit bottom.

Coming clean with you now, I wanted very much to be completely off antidepressants upon completion of this book. What joy it would be to talk about depression recovery and note that I didn't need any more meds. Alas, it seems I need to take a page from my own book here. I've discovered once more the hard way, that I am chemically unbalanced.

"What are you trying to prove?" my doctor will ask. "If you were a diabetic and you woke up one day and decided you were strong enough not to take your insulin, you'd go into a seizure. Clinical depression is very much like diabetes."

The question for me is, how many times will I make a stupid choice based on what I wish were true as opposed to accepting the reality of my chemical makeup? The definition of insanity ironically comes to mind: doing the same thing over and over again and expecting different results.

❧

Sometimes the church and mental-health issues are like water and oil. They do not mix well.

❧

Avoiding Medication

For those who suffer with bipolar disorder or schizophrenia, staying on medication is essential for survival. Bipolar depressives often stop taking medication when they feel better. Because of the nature of this type of depression, when the highs hit, there is a strong temptation to throw the pills away. Over and over again horrible setbacks occur when someone goes "cold turkey."

The following e-mail is from a wonderful hospice nurse. She describes the reaction of a young woman who went off her meds during a manic phase.

> Ann was in a crisis. She couldn't sleep, was overanxious and paranoid about her medication, so she stopped taking it. She was found in a Wal-Mart, where she had wandered about all night in a daze. When she came home, she cut her hair off, started crying, and was making no sense. She could talk for a few minutes but was irrational.
>
> Her mother had been down a similar path of mental illness and didn't want her daughter to be hospitalized, so Ann was discouraged from getting the help she desperately needed.
>
> She is a young, 30-ish mother of a 6-year-old and has been married only a short time. Her husband doesn't know what to do with her, so he chooses to avoid her. His family thinks she has gone crazy and is concerned about the welfare of their grandchild.
>
> She was told by many well-meaning Christians that she was being tortured by demons and should seek God more and have more faith, not medical treatment.
>
> She is utterly confused.
>
> We intervened and convinced her to go back on her medication. Fortunately, manic depression is a chronic illness that can be treated, but it must be clearly, thoroughly explained to family and friends. If the patient stops the medication and cycles out of control, the depressive state starts all over again.

> Sometimes the church and mental-health issues are
> like water and oil. They do not mix well. Both sides need
> to understand the other. There's a bridge across the river
> that needs to be built.

～

While working on this book, I found myself sitting one day at a national chain store waiting three hours for a simple oil change. I often strike up conversations with strangers I meet on the road, and we end up talking about what brought us to the place we are. As I sat, frustrated by a simple procedure that was taking hours, I experienced, to use the cliché—a blessing in disguise.

First, I met a youth group stranded by a tire blowout. Then a couple of young men in their 20s trying to head home to Tampa, followed by two young moms, and finally a handsome officer stationed in the local army division nearby. With my laptop and research materials on depression scattered about me, I was asked about my work. Hesitant to discuss the topic, I was astonished to see how depression became the common denominator of each conversation.

I was flabbergasted to hear one of the 20-something young men perk up and tell me how he'd been suffering from depression for years and had finally found a medication that gave him relief. At first the doctor had tried something too strong, but this young man had been relieved to finally meet a doctor who had him on a minimal amount of antidepressants, which gave him a balanced view of life. He offered this information without hiding anything, and with an air of freedom.

Soon after the young man and his friend exited, the army officer, who had overheard our conversation, asked me to please continue writing this book. His young wife was dealing with a severe bout of depression, having lost several members of her family to suicide.

"Please tell the caregivers not to be afraid." He looked at me straight on. "And let them know that some medications have side effects for at time, but it's worth the relief that comes to the one you love."

I left my oil change dazed by the encounters with these strangers who were dealing with depression—and committed more than ever to be a voice of clarity and encouragement about this disease.

Antidepressants and Christians

Modern science has stumbled and fallen and often failed us. Each of us have choices to make about how to respond to options offered by the current medical/physiological treatments for body and soul. Progress comes to us as God allows, slowly, graciously, and never without an appropriate amount of healthy skepticism.

Still, the walking dead are not just in old black-and-white movies. They stagger through life in living color, terrified and alone, many sitting in churches all across the world, longing for help.

Attempting to suppress depression that might otherwise respond to medication can lead to substance abuse, rage, homes filled with unrest and misery, reclusive mental invalids, and death…all suffered under the cloak of pride. Anyone pressured to not seek medical attention should find a friend or family member who will explain the realities of depression and the importance of the sound advice of a professional.

One friend wrote to me,

> I didn't tell anyone at church I was suffering. How could I explain to someone that the joy of the Lord wasn't my strength? One time, when I tried to explain my sadness, someone told me to "just rebuke that depression!" *If only it were that easy,* I thought. Did they really think I was enjoying feeling this way?
>
> Ironically, I was assigned to write an article on depression for a Christian magazine. When I was conducting interviews, I felt a lightening in my spirit. I made

an appointment with a wonderful doctor and had to fight myself not to cancel it. When he confirmed the diagnosis I was in a depression, I almost collapsed with relief.

We discussed various treatments, and I left his office with samples of a gentle antidepressant...and the understanding it might take several weeks before I felt better.

About a week later, I told my husband, "I don't know if it's the medicine, or what, but I feel better."

He told me that he noticed the change as well, and I continued to feel more normal with each day. Later my husband told the doctor that it was like experiencing a resurrection.

⌒

The Minirth-Meier Clinic has published a book, now in its third or fourth edition, called *Happiness Is a Choice: The Symptoms, Causes, and Cures of Depression.* Initially the title put me off—*way* off. *What do you mean, I can choose happiness?* I thought resentfully. *Is this another cliché-ridden book about pulling myself up by my bootstraps?* Still, I purchased it. I began to devour the text, which was filled with medical, psychiatric, and spiritual truths. Clutching the book each day, knowing I was taking three medications to try and get my act together, I trembled at the possibility of hitting on a chapter advising *no meds.*

My fears were unfounded. Instead I found words like these:

A century ago, a number of Christians thought it was a sin to wear glasses, or "devil's eyes," as they called them. Their reasoning was, "If God wanted you to be able to see, He would have given you good vision." Even after penicillin was discovered, many Christians died of pneumonia because they wanted to trust God alone and not medications. We know of several Christians who have died...because they refused to have cancer surgically removed.

Technically, mankind has come a long way; he has even walked on the moon. But when it comes to common sense, whether it be Christians or non-Christians, we have not advanced a great deal from where we were during the Dark Ages.[2]

Minirth and Meier go on to describe their theory on antidepressants and hospitalizations if necessary. They praise God for new treatments available to so many, who do not need to suffer in silence or feel suicidal. They ask,

Should antidepressants ever be used? Of course, under certain circumstances. Which option is the most spiritual if the patient has four children at home who have been hurting for months because of his depression? Which option is the most spiritual if suicide is a real possibility, a possibility that would leave children fatherless (or motherless) and with deep emotional scars?[3]

Along with medical chemical treatment, there is a safe, risk-free, completely free source of natural chemicals—our bodies, which produce them when we exercise. All right, I know that most people suffering with depression cannot imagine walking to the mailbox, much less doing a workout at the local Y. But I am suggesting only the simplest of exercises. Any kind of walking, anywhere, will not only get your physical body out of hibernation from the world, but the smallest amounts of exercise will release good endorphins, mood messengers sent to your brain as comfort and relief. If you cannot go outside, then just do simple stretches in your home. *Any* physical movement will help the medication and your mental state.

A Matter of Life and Death for Christians Too

Depression is a fight for life. It's serious and must not be minimized.

During my daughter's senior year in a private Christian high school, two young people attempted suicide. One, tragically, succeeded. The handsome captain of the football team—a popular, sharp young senior, went home one afternoon, slipped into his bedroom, and pulled the trigger of a shotgun.

His parents, devastated, nevertheless took the time and great effort to go out and speak to groups of high school seniors who had known their son. They spoke of how he loved God, but had made a bad choice.

At the memorial service, however, a well-meaning but ill-advised pastor made the comment, "Do you wonder what God said to this young man when he arrived in heaven? I believe God said to him, 'Well done, my good and faithful servant!'"

You've got to be kidding me!

First of all, there were sitting in the church—that very day—young teenagers who were also contemplating suicide. As I see it, this pastor just gave anyone thinking of taking their life a God-stamped endorsement for a bad choice.

I cannot know what God might have conveyed to this precious young man as he entered heaven. I might imagine that the compassionate, all-knowing, and merciful voice of the Father might have said, "I love you so much! I had much more for you to experience there on earth. Plans for you, plans you will not know now—but My love for you will never change." The young man will never know what life might have offered if he had been able to fight off the desire to kill himself. "If-only" thoughts litter the lives of the depressed, and they make me want to drag out my soapbox.

Suicide is the most cruel act anyone could commit against those who love them. But I also know personally what it's like to sit and wonder how it would feel not to hurt any more. My children most surely gave me the will to fight for my sanity. But I hear far too many times of pastors, young children, people of all ages and socioeconomic backgrounds, who find life so dark that they end their time here by their own hand.

They Could Have Been Helped

Renée Coates Scheidt tells the story of her husband Chuck's journey through manic depression in her book *Songs of the Night*. Chuck was a youth pastor, a charming man filled with dreams and a passion for life. When he and Renée married and started their family, they had no idea how depression would ravage their home.

> Manic-depression was still an unknown term to us. It would be ten years later when we discovered this was the cause of the emotional mood swings Chuck fought all of his adult life.[4]

Chuck and Renée bravely sought prayer from their church home for the unexplainable dark days Chuck battled. Doctors tried therapies and counseling, and Chuck was told it would be a long time for him to recover. Prayer vigils were held, and Renée wondered what biblical truth they hadn't uncovered that would release her husband from his depression. "No matter how many Bible verses we quoted on the victory we have in Christ or how hard Chuck worked to apply them, the depression never left for long."[5]

Renée reflects on the lack of antidepressant treatment:

> The chemical imbalance which caused Chuck's manic-depression needed proper medication. No amount of "right thinking and right actions" would correct the physiological illness. Working in conjunction with medical means, these elements can be very effective. One without the other, however, is not always enough...It's like having only two legs on a three-legged stool—very wobbly and unable to support any amount of weight.[6]

By the time Chuck at last received medical antidepressant therapy, the doctors had a very difficult time finding the exact medication that would effectively transition him into health. After eight weeks of hospitalization, he was sent home, but Renée felt instinctively he was not ready. He immediately began to show signs of drifting back into the darkness.

The last day of his life, Chuck's symptoms were clear: lack of sleep, loss of appetite, restlessness, asking to see a doctor…and then he disappeared for the last time. He was found in a nearby lot, mangled by a gunshot to the head. The doctor had answered Renée's frantic page. But it was too late.

Desperate for a word from God, Renée remembered a Bible verse she'd heard in college. Stunned friends and family listened to the trembling voice of this widowed, 32-year-old mother of two young girls as she spoke at her husband's memorial service: "Thank you, God, that You have said, 'Precious in Your sight is the death of Your saint.'" After decades of watching her husband fight for his life—misdiagnosed, untreated by medication until it was too late—she thanked God for the father of her children. "Thank you that he doesn't hurt anymore. He fought long and hard. Thank you, God, for receiving him into heaven."[7]

As Renée put it so well, "Chuck's problems were not due to a lack of spirituality or some sin in his life. He actually had a physical problem beyond the realm of his control."[8]

Finding Permission

Julie Barnhill, author, speaker, and precious friend of my heart, shares about the "scorched places" each of us have in our lives. The times when life falls apart and we cave in with it. The places that hurt so much we throw a mental blanket over them to keep them covered, afraid if we move too close, they will devour us. Her scorched place is the knowledge she was adopted. Separated from her birth siblings, fantasizing about even the smallest details of how her birth mother looked, a gnawing need to find her roots brought her crashing down. Dealing with relationships with members of her estranged birth family brought on a depression defined by loss. She tells of the result:

> It was supernatural grace, coupled with the practical, medicinal grace of antidepressants, which brought about my ultimate healing. I believe without shame or hesitancy that God directs physicians and pharmacists as sovereignly as he does pastors and Christian authors! His lavish grace is not limited to the ethereal but is evidenced in the very chemical compounds of our bodies and medicinal aids![9]

Publicly, one might hear Julie let out a fantastic laugh and admit, "Prozac is my new best friend!"

It's not with pleasure or pride that I am occasionally called to accountability by my husband's question, "Sweetheart, are you taking your medications?" He knows me so well, and he knows I've foolishly stopped my meds before. If Brent sees me approaching a cliff he will lovingly confront me. Shaking off a tinge of failure, I know it's a valid question. Without staying on a regular cycle of medication, I'm not sure who would wake up in my house each day! (Brent says I can be "a great bunch of girls"—his attempt at lightening me up. But he has a point.)

To dispel any final myths, let me be blunt.

Antidepressants do not make me high—not even close! There is no rush...no thrilling vibes...no living in la-la land. Antidepressants allow me to see life for what it is. The medications allow me to make focused decisions, and to be a wife, mother, and friend to the best of my ability. They make sleep now possible for me, although it's still difficult.

↜

Antidepressants are not the be-all-and-end-all solution to depression. For many, however, they radically improve the recovery process. Along with spiritual encouragement of the soul, the body needs the chance to heal.

With your stretcher-bearers praying, explore medical treatment with a doctor who understands depression. Many times this can be your family doctor. In rare instances, psychiatrists are recommended.

There is no shame in reaching out for all available aid.

Your life is worth every ounce of energy, time, investment, and investigation spent on saving it.

God so loved you that He gave His Son to bring you life...not just in the "sweet bye-and-bye"...but now, right where you are.

Keep climbing.

~

I believe in God and I believe in the sun. Not because I can see them, but because by them I can see everything else.

C.S. LEWIS

Now the greater our knowledge of our own misery, the more profound will be our confidence in the goodness and mercy of God, for mercy and misery are so closely connected that the one cannot be exercised without the other.

FRANCIS DE SALES
The Art of Loving God

PART THREE

Starting to Climb Again

9

CONFESSIONS
OF THE HEART

I hate being a statistic. I hate the term "broken home."
The reality is, however, that even though I do come from
one of these so-called homes, the healing process has
produced a young woman who is continually aware of
and amazed at God's unconditional love and faith-
fulness.

This paragraph was penned by my daughter, Courtney, during
her junior year in college. My oldest child, a feisty, inquisitive
beauty, was six years old when her father and I were divorced. "I
was riding my bicycle around my driveway with my best friend,
the day my life changed forever," Courtney writes. "My parents
called me inside. The three of us stood in the entryway, and they
crouched down to tell me, 'Courtney, we are going to get a
divorce.'"

I took Courtney to "counsel," kicking and screaming all the
way to the office doors, when she was young. She let me know, as
she will, how she felt about therapy. She was not cooperative and

never seemed to benefit much from the sessions. The anger in her came out in dribs and drabs. Yet she learned to keep her frustration at bay for many years.

Fast-forward to her senior year in high school. My tall, beautiful, overachiever daughter stood before me, and much to my shock, requested time with a counselor. "I've carried around so many things…I don't want to go any further, into college, or anywhere without resolving what's happening in me."

The Story

Now a journalism major, Courtney spells things out in a paper titled "A Broken Home Mended":

> I made straight A's, I performed starring roles in various plays and musicals, I started for the varsity volleyball team, I was even voted Best All Around by classmates. Yet my attempts at being perfect didn't succeed in covering up the hurt little girl inside of me. Reality can't always be masked or forgotten, no matter how powerful the distraction. I used some very creative tactics to try and pile on coats and coats of fresh paint over a cracking wall. Eventually, it became too heavy…

When she asked for a counselor, I picked up the phone and immediately made appointments for a series of sessions with a professional I trusted to hear her heart and know what to do with the broken pieces.

Proverbs 11:14 came to mind: "Where there is no guidance the people fall, but in abundance of counselors there is victory" (NASB).

Bring on the abundance of counselors!

I had spent many years as a single parent to Courtney and her younger brother, Graham. They had witnessed a very human struggling mom, trying in very flawed ways to love them well. God knows I longed to be a mother like the ones from a "whole" home. Though ours was broken by the world's definition, God allowed the three of us a sweet, precious, safe home together in spite of our circumstances.

Watching my daughter choose therapy was sobering, knowing how much she disliked the process. I wanted to shower her with awards for courage, while my heart was torn over the loss she had carried for so long. (It's no secret that divorce is hated because of what happens to the innocent children it affects. No matter what leads you to its door, it just plain stinks.)

Courtney's counselor began to address the childhood pain from the divorce in our family. "I said it was fine because, after all, that wasn't my problem," Courtney admitted to her therapist. "I became such a pro at denying the hurt that I had even tricked myself. It took me a while to finally reach deep down and realize how much pain I had buried." She saw the counselor every week for ten sessions, and worked with serious determination to prepare to leave home for college without taking unnecessary baggage.

"A Summer of Healing" is the name of a picture she painted that year. It shows a huge tree with a large branch framing the top of the painting. From the tree hangs a chain holding an assortment of heavy objects. The chain is breaking and the pieces are falling. On the opposite side of the painting is a heart, broken, with tears falling down onto a bed of flowers on the verge of blossoming.

"My counselor guided me through the typical stages of grief," Courtney explains.

> We began with my denial. I started to sort through the lies I had told myself. I believed I wasn't a good daughter, that it was my fault I was needy, that I had to carry the burden of the divorce. The tears would flow without apparent reason, but I knew it was all part of the process. I was going to be free. Once I realized how I had held myself captive, I began to let God become my true Father. I let him come into those dark places that I was ashamed of, and heal them.

Typing these words, I feel tears falling from my eyes. My stomach is in a knot, and I am fighting back a dark shadow of familiar guilt. But beyond a mother's reaction to her daughter's pain, I see a young woman of who I am so proud. Courtney has never backed down from a challenge, even if it meant she might have to fight in the trenches for a time.

Stormy Mitchell, a tremendous friend and a business associate, remarked, "When you come up against a painful experience, like Courtney has done over and over again, you have three choices. You can run from the pain, you can deny the pain, or you can run into the pain and allow yourself to become stronger by overcoming it. She chooses the hard path, but look at the beauty of her character!"

My steel-magnolia daughter truly embodies the sentiment, "That which does not kill us makes us stronger."

During her second year in college, Courtney met with my medical doctor, and we discussed her anxiety and the possibility of depression. Ever the overachiever, Courtney had been on the dean's list with incredible grades, all while pushing hard through her volleyball commitments. It was taking a toll, and I asked my doctor—a godly person I highly respect—whether my daughter might be a candidate for depression. Courtney and I both sighed and pouted a little, but agreed that she has my DNA and my predisposition to seeing the glass half-empty. A very small amount of a gentle antidepressant was prescribed, and it completely changed her ability to cope. She had already done the counseling—now the medication made everything work together.

Facing the Reality of Personal Pain

Counseling—wise, godly, direct, truthful guidance—is the third area of depression recovery. First, you have spiritually asked God to be your *everything,* and your "stretcher-bearers" are praying. Resting your weakened self on His strength allows you to seek medical help if necessary. With your spiritual heart focused on worshiping God and proper medication helping you into healthy eating, sleeping, and work patterns, it is then critical to investigate the root of the loss that triggered your depression.

However, I cannot emphasize enough that without a spiritual regrouping, and medication giving the physical and mental strength to move ahead, counseling should not be an option. In

> Counseling is nearly impossible to face unless the symptoms of depression are under control through a sense of trusting God. Spiritual, physical, and emotional healing work hand-in-hand.

my opinion, one cannot replace the other. Prayer in and of itself will not necessarily cure depression. Medication can become a crutch if the center of our lives is not focused on God's will. And counseling is nearly impossible to face unless the symptoms of depression are under control through a sense of trusting God. Spiritual, physical, and emotional healing work hand-in-hand.

"To obtain and apply to one's life good-quality Christian counseling is synonymous with discipleship."[1] Discipleship is learning, becoming a student...studying healing from the Great Healer. Counselors guide us into becoming effective students of life, into understanding the abundance of life Jesus died to give us.

As Courtney has done, as I have done, as many others who've suffered depression have done, we've gotten down to the nitty-gritty reality of our personal pain through counseling. We've asked ourselves tough questions:

- How do you define joy?
- What does it mean to be happy?
- What expectations did you have for life that fell through?

- What loss upon loss was the last straw for your broken heart?

- What injustice have you suffered from childhood situations you may have had no control over? What injustice have you felt responsible for or been ashamed to face?

- What part of being human, in a fallen garden, has overwhelmed you and brought on a depression?

Mike Mason writes of his search for lasting joy in the book *Champagne for the Soul:*

> When cornered, we have to look at all the options and find the way out. We have to know how to outwit the heebie-jeebies, how to think faster than our blackest thought. We must be able to slip through the nooses of condemnation, lethargy, self-pity, confusions. Joy may seem to be an upbeat sort of feeling, but the direction of joy isn't always up. Often to be joyful we must go down through the noise of racing thoughts, down through the swirling chaos of circumstances, down through the deceptive appearances of life, down into the still waters and green pastures at the heart's core.[2]

Sometimes, to find joy, we must open up to someone trained to help us recover the "wily" willingness to believe we can be happy again. There is an amazing miracle that occurs when we speak out loud about our deepest fears, the darkest moments, the most difficult conversations or events. When we dare to open up to just one other trusted person, when the secret is out...it begins to lose its power. Counselors are gifted in the healing process of the soul, as doctors are gifted in healing the body.

In the safety of a good counselor's office, the root causes of loss can be sifted through and put in perspective. The horrific feelings of shame or disappointment or fear that were buried so meticulously in our psyche that depression erupted can be exposed. It's time to allow God to touch the most wounded places.

Sharing your sorrow, your thoughts, and your feelings is the most effective way to keep from surrendering to your depression. As your depression is released, you can open your hands to receive new emotions to replace the depression. You were so filled with negative emotions that nothing else could get in. Now, there is room...[3]

An Ally and a Safety Net

Depression has been defined as anger turned in on oneself.

Do you have unresolved anger at someone, alive or perhaps not here anymore, and haven't known what to do with the feelings?

In my case, I was angriest at myself. The darkness of depression shed light on the mystery of my turmoil. I blamed myself for not being someone I couldn't possibly be. I was human, weak, and full of sin. What a discovery! I was human, weak, full of sin—and saved in spite of myself by a God who loved life back into me.

Depression can be your ally.

It can serve to release you from pain.

It's not my personal favorite choice for a wake-up call, but for me, it has been an unmistakable memo from my body—a cry for help.

Courtney has been on a volleyball scholarship throughout her college career. It requires relentless training year-round and daily commitments for travel on top of her class load. In her freshman year, she would call me nearly every day on the way to the gym.

"Tell me I can do this, Mommy...just tell me I can do this," she would say, holding back tears and reaching out for help.

"You can do this, baby," wanna-be-brave mom would reply. "Just this afternoon, just today, you can do this. Don't think about tomorrow. Just go in there today and do what you can."

As a parent, I often feel like a middle-aged safety net! The older my children are, the more they are out walking the tightrope of life without my hands to keep them balanced. Now more than ever, it's about prayer and being a voice of hope. The winds can blow wild and wreak havoc with the tightrope. My phone may ring any hour, day or night, and I will hear from the other end, "Just tell me I'll be all right. Tell me I can do this." (And to my Father I whisper, *Tell me I can do this life thing! It's hard, it's scary, it's full of sinkholes and muck up to my ears. If I fall, will You be there?*)

꙳

Good counselors are medicine for the depressed soul. "You can do this" is the subtext for every session. "For today, you can look at what is required of you, and God will give you exactly what you need, and not one iota more, to face your day." A solid counselor is a skilled ally, standing by you as you air out the deftly hidden toxin-filled rooms in your heart.

> Each of us has an unfolding story, constructed of past issues from things that are not of our choosing. Each of us, granted the time and the courage, could expose multiple layers of past and present neediness, triumphs and losses.[4]

Counselors are the safety net during the exploration of our broken places. They are the host who skillfully invites the healing power of Jesus into the darkness we are terrified to face alone. They are trained to see warning signs for a change in medication, or to be a representative voice of the truths of God's love. They are, crudely put, a safe place to spill your guts.

Does it hurt?

It hurts like hell.

But like a baby's first cry after inhaling air into lungs that have only known fluid, it's a pain that promises life.

Secrets are defeated.

Truth wins the day.

Over time, pain begins to take a back seat to joy.

C.S. Lewis described the process thus: "...as if the lifting of sorrow removed a great barrier."

A Place to Find Courage to Embrace Life

Courtney describes making her decision for therapy:

> I will not say it was easy. The process required more courage than I thought I could muster up, and it hurt more than anything else I have ever been through. But God doesn't promise us easiness in this life, and I am overwhelmingly grateful for the strength that my pain has produced. God granted me beauty for ashes.
>
> I chose to uncover the ugly wound, to let it breathe, to let it heal. When a person breaks a bone or muscle, it grows back stronger. And so it has been with my heart. I have turned from hollow promises and people and lifted my face up to breathe.

Frederick Buechner, the world-renowned author and speaker, was 12 years old when his beloved father committed suicide. The family found him closed in their garage, his car running. This young husband and father had taken his own life, unfortunately where his two sons would find him.

The oldest son Frederick's defiant choice to embrace life in all its pain and holiness is breathtaking. Buechner's writings shout from each page the sanctity of telling the truth, staring down our demons, and finding the face of Jesus in the sea of humanity around us. The son of a man who took himself out of life, Buechner has thrown himself headlong *into* life, defining his humanity with transparent reverence: "Listen to your life," he writes in *Now and Then*.

> See it for the fathomless mystery that it is. In the boredom and pain of it no less than in the excitement and gladness; touch, taste, smell your way to the holy and hidden heart of it because in the last analysis all moments are key moments, and life itself is grace.[5]

His words tackle despair by reflecting on the insistent, merciful, besotten love of God—continually wooing each man, woman, and child to an intersection with Himself: "The unflagging lunacy of God. The unending seaminess of man. The meeting between them that is always a matter of life or death and usually both,"[6] as Buechner observes in his book *Wishful Thinking*.

Godly, Christian counseling is such an intersection. The wild love of God meets man in the brokenness of his human condition through men and women of faith who have taken up the cross of studying the psychology of the mind. In the matter of life and death during a depression, we are given a choice. To fight for our lives, with the help of professionals, or to give in to defeat. If we are willing to find a way back into life again, counselors can guide us through the landmines of our darkest hours and diffuse the mystery of our madness.

A Place to Embrace Truth

There have been days when I truly feared I was going mad. There have been moments when everything around me looked like loss. And I felt I had nothing to give anyone, and that I was of little use to my family in particular. Lies swirl around my thought process when I get into this sort of mood, and I speak out loud the words of Philippians 4:6-7:

> Do not fret or have any anxiety about anything, but in every circumstance and in everything, by prayer and petition (definite requests), with thanksgiving, continue to make your wants known to God. And God's peace [shall be yours, that tranquil state of a soul assured of its salvation through Christ, and so fearing nothing from God and being content with its earthly lot of whatever sort that is, that peace] which transcends all understanding shall garrison and mount guard over your hearts and minds in Christ Jesus.[7]

God will mount a garrison, a legion of His armored guard to watch over my heart and mind if I will only ask. I was not created to fear but to have a spirit of power and of love and, as Timothy notes the comforting promise, "of a sound mind."

My time under several counselors' care was invaluable to my healing from depression. Together we peeled back layers of my life, almost like cleaning out an old shed that had been padlocked far too long. I discovered several areas that are trigger points for me—places in my heart that continually require the truth of God's mercy washing over them, reminding me of who I am as His daughter.

During counseling I began to throw out some of the garbage I'd attached to my self-image. I began to surrender to the reality of being human—having limitations, and respecting what those limitations were. All my life I'd heard, "All things are possible with Christ Jesus." With frenetic vigor I altered the translation of this truth to mean that I could force possibility into impossible scenarios, without taking into consideration the "free will" variable of other people.

The guidance of my counselors clearly, gently helped open my eyes to the difference between having Christ give me His strength and relying on my own. I couldn't make everyone else's choices for them, and I had many lessons on forgiveness and grace to learn.

Hesitations

Is counseling expensive?

It's not possible to put a price tag on the worth of one human psyche...soul. Jesus died for each one as His personal gift to all of mankind. In my case, the process was worth every penny, every mile driven, every appointment that usually brought on a few waves of nausea.

Does it take forever to get to the bottom of things?

No.

When you're depressed, you are already at the bottom. All you need do is let go of needless pride, and open up and take a clear, honest look at your life.

Any counselor worth their salt is dedicated to getting you into their office, into sound mental health, and out of their office in good time. Being stuck in the inability to leave counseling is as unhealthy as being afraid to seek help in the first place.

Do not let fear stand in your way. And if you cannot afford to hire someone, then ask for help at local churches, which often have professional therapists on staff, along with offering access to support groups. God is raising up many Christian counseling centers.

If you are a church seeking confirmation about whether or not to start up such a program, no matter how small, I implore you to do so. "Loneliness was the first thing God saw in all creation that he said was not good. Be on the lookout for someone who is suffering its miseries."[8]

A Place to Confess

> Confess your sins to each other and pray for each other so God can heal you. When a believing person prays, great things happen.[9]

Confession and prayer with a counselor is deeply healing! To tell your story, your very own, personal, warts-and-all story to another person—one who is not going to judge you or make you feel condemned, but wants to help you sort through your life—can spark a heart revolution!

Probably the most therapeutic part of psychotherapy

is that the despairing individual who feels rejected, hopeless, and alone has access to the patience, understanding and concern of a counselor in confidentiality and privacy. If the counselor can sufficiently meet the patient's needs by suggesting corrective measures the counselee can take to change his thinking patterns, counseling can often provide a very meaningful crutch upon which the depressed person may lean.[10]

God has used wise counsel throughout biblical history to awaken the need of His people to return to Him, discover His amazing grace, and see the reality of their choices through the healing power of confession.

God used the words of Nathan, a wise-hearted counselor, to release King David from captivity to the torment of his sin. David took another man's wife to sleep with him and then had her husband killed on the battlefield.

In the second book of Samuel, Nathan tells David the story of a heartless man who took what was not his. When asked what should happen to such a man, David replied, "Death!" Nathan then said that this man represented David himself.

The king felt the piercing words fall upon him, and as the newborn son of his adulterous union lay extremely ill, David begged God to forgive him, confessed that He had sinned first and foremost against the Lord, and requested a new heart and right spirit replace his darkness. All the while, David waited to see if his young son would live or die, refusing to eat or drink. The people watching his behavior thought David might commit suicide when word came that the baby had died.

Yet in an astounding act of faith in the character of God, after the news came, David washed himself, ate, and went in to be with his wife, Bathsheba. He knew that his relationship with God was again clear, unhindered, pure, and on track. On that very night, David and Bathsheba conceived another child who would one day build a temple to God and rule Israel—a son named Solomon.

Without the guiding counsel of Nathan, David might not have

been able to reconnect with God as the center of his heart. His grief might have eaten away at the core of his faith. But God is merciful, and He brings counsel to any person willing to hear—words of grace to move us on and out of depression.

In David's wrestling heart, I see the heart of myself and of all mankind when we are too close to our situation to see Truth crying out. After my divorce, I wanted love, I wanted remarriage so desperately that it clouded my judgment and took over the center of my heart...God was displaced. I couldn't understand why my spirit was so defeated and my life looked hopeless. Counseling gave me perspective and the tools I needed to get my priorities back in line.

Though counseling is never a substitute for time with God, good counseling ushers in the Holy Spirit of the Lord and encourages the heart to believe that hope is alive and well.

Healed Scars

Recently I met an intriguing, deep woman who shared her story of recovery from extreme stress and depression with me. In her book, *Freed by Faith*, this lovely, vintage lady of Christ writes,

> Certain areas of our lives need emotional healing by the power of Jesus Christ which is given to us by the Holy Spirit. Psychiatry can begin a degree of healing by probing into the past...but only the Holy Spirit can remove the scars. Psychiatry helps for a while, but only Jesus heals permanently.[11]

Yes, and amen.

Only Jesus the Ultimate Healer heals permanently—in ways as varied as each unique human soul knit together by God's hands.

But I also contend that the scars from depression, although healed, will remain. I am grateful for the desolation of my depression because it brought me face-to-face with a Christ I didn't know existed. How many times did I feel so weepy that I thought even God must be sick to death of me? Yet I felt His compassionate arms around me, the empathy of His eyes looking into me through my tears. At last I began to glimpse the scars of depression Jesus took to the cross for me.

He was not repulsed. He understood.

As Christ emerged from his burial tomb, he appeared physically to His family of disciples. Doubting Thomas could scarcely believe his eyes. Jesus, beaten beyond recognition, bleeding to death naked on a cross for all to see, stood smiling before him three days later, asking for something to eat.

Doubting God's love is a natural response to depression. Doubt does not imply that you have given up on God—but like Job, Jonah, Peter, John the Baptist, and Thomas, you fall into the ranks of the many warriors of faith who have wondered, *What is God up to? Why does He allow suffering?*

> Those who believe that they believe in God, but without any passion in their heart, any anguish of mind, without uncertainty, without doubt, without an element of despair even in their consolation, believe only in the God-idea, not in God.[12]

How did Jesus use His pain for good—the wounds to His hands, His feet, the place the sword was thrust into His side? Christ took the hand of Thomas and allowed him to feel His scars and to see what God had done through His resurrected body.

Yes, "even the resurrected Christ kept his scars,"[13] as Philip Yancey notes.

As you find counsel, reveal your losses, surrender them into the hands of God, and discover the healing power of forgiveness and the infinite grace of Jesus, you also may learn to treasure your scars. They serve to remind any of us who deal with depression that we are learning to praise God in the dark as well as the light. We have survived another day, and by the mercy of Christ, will not be defeated.

There is a moment in each day
that Satan cannot find.

~

WILLIAM BLAKE

10

UNLIKELY COUSINS: ANGER AND FORGIVENESS

For 15 years, I watched my earthly father suffer from the cruel disease of Alzheimer's. God graciously took Daddy home on July 1, 2004. He graduated with honors, and we celebrated his life. I was given the rare privilege of a "Sacred Farewell"—praying, singing, and literally speaking glory over my daddy as he left this earth. Lying in bed beside him, I sang hymns, made up songs, read Scripture, and looked into his eyes, predicting he would soon dance with the angels. His hand and mine were intertwined as he took his last breath, and I fell to the ground praising God and rejoicing. My father didn't have to suffer any more.

Daddy was a gentle man in the truest sense of the word, a gentleman of the South. He was also a brilliant man, chosen by the Army to work on the testing of the atomic bomb, and later a quiet man, who loved to study blueprints of computers for fun. Daddy was uniquely witty, gracious, astute, and godly, and was loving in his own way.

The "in his own way" was the hard part for me.

Daddy loved me, but he was never able to tell me verbally or show me any physical affection. My very first memory is from when I was five years old. Dad sat reading the paper in the living room, and I crawled around the back of the curtains, watching him, wanting him to see me. I left the room and asked my mother, "Does Daddy love me?" I was too afraid to ask him directly. And the uncertain answer to the question hovered over me as I grew into womanhood.

When clinical depression brought me to my knees after a divorce, failed relationships, and a ministry broken apart by betrayals, I began to explore the creases and folds of my heart to see what might be hidden there. One of the pieces of my soul's puzzle was a lifetime of longing for my daddy's love.

At first I felt guilty about having unresolved questions.

But I realized it was something that had affected my choices in marriage, men, and how I viewed myself as a woman. If my daddy did not seem interested in me, then why would any healthy man love me? And if I didn't value myself as a woman of God, then what did I have to bring to a relationship?

Mom's love for me was over the top. I was her ace, the one she bragged on as I won awards and lived out a life in the spotlight— singing, speaking, and performing music and theater she admired. Daddy would come to events and never say a word to me afterward. Maybe Mom said enough for everyone, but I wished I could have heard my father's approval.

During my divorce, Daddy and I became closer than we'd ever been. He drove carpool, moved furniture in and out of my house, fixed anything that went wonky, and showed me love by his actions. Still, Daddy didn't believe I would ever marry again. "Why would anyone marry you, as old as you are with two children?" he asked once with acrid naïvete.

If my own father didn't believe in my womanhood or in the power of God to do what He thought best for me, then how could I have any hope?

Anger lurked beneath the surface of my heart for years. Anger showed up and demanded to be reckoned with during my depression.

I could turn the anger in on my body again, or I could face it and let it go. With counsel from friends and professionals and urging from the Spirit of God, I chose to take the bull by the horns and deal with my anger once and for all.

Expressions of Anger

For me, a child growing up in a Christian home, the expression of anger was not smiled on. In fact, it was simply not tolerated. I am not alone in this.

> Many parents discourage their children from sharing their angry feelings, even appropriately. In fact, some parents punish their children for sharing normal angry feelings appropriately. Many of you probably learned to fear your anger because being aware and sharing your anger resulted in rejection and punishment. You may have grown up in a legalistic church that taught you all anger is sin.[1]

Depression is often unresolved anger turned inward.

I have come to believe that childhood anger expressed appropriately could prevent a myriad of adult train wrecks.

No wonder so many Christians suffer silently with despair. Many of us were taught from childhood that anger is a sin. Christians are not supposed to be angry. We do not allow our children to express anger.

I have come to believe that childhood anger expressed appropriately could prevent a myriad of adult train wrecks.

As parents, we must meet the challenge of finding a healthy way to allow our children to express their rage at a world out of control. In no way would I suggest that children be given free rein without discipline or free rein to behave in a disrespectful manner. But a healthy release of anger can keep a child from mental and physical disorders.

Parents' expectations, especially those in a faith-based home, are usually quite high. Well-meaning parents take their children to church, Christian schools, and youth-group meetings where the message comes across loud and clear: "Be good—be godly people who make good choices, good grades, good friends…so you'll have success in the eyes of man and God."

So what happens when a child feels excessively blamed, judged, or even disappointed in themselves?

What does one do with the simple frustrations of living in a fallen world?

What happens when the grace of the cross is buried under judgment?

I was not allowed to express any anger as a child. That was coupled with expectations that I would be a stellar achiever. Knowing deep down I might fail, wondering if my daddy loved me, and hoping I could live up to God's and my family's expectations made me an emotionally fragile little girl. Migraine headaches were an ongoing part of my life from the early age of six.

One of the clearest memories I have is of a lie I told in the third grade. My teacher asked if anyone had put their coat on the wrong rack in the closet, and I emphatically said, "No, ma'am!"—all the while knowing I'd committed the "crime."

Arriving home, I went into my room, closed the door, and wrote a letter to God. I begged Him to forgive me for telling a lie. Though a forgiving God was foreign to me, still I wrote the letter, hoping for a break. Slashing marks in my diary, the only safe place to express rage, I let out the anger and fear bottled up in me, tears staining the pages written to heaven without a postmark. If only I had confessed to the teacher I'd told a lie and believed that sins would be forgiven…If only I had known that injustice, failing, and getting back up again were just a part of life…

If only I had had a sense of the grace of God.

⌐◝

As I look at how Christ responded to life here on earth, I am relieved to see His anger at the injustice of the world. Jesus declared that when we see Him, we see God. In seeing the Word made flesh, we find many moments when God in Jesus—Emmanuel—is passionate. He is livid, He agonizes over the lost and sin-filled garden. He does not sin, yet His rage is apparent many times over in the brief, powerful records of His life on earth.

Jesus sees people being taken advantage of, quite literally being robbed and charged to the max for offerings during the Passover.[2] His anger causes Him to turn over tables and storm through the temple in anguish. This was a place where God was to be met and worshiped. It had been turned into a place where the highest price was asked for the sacrifices offered.

Christ's impassioned words against legalism and the law-bound religious leaders of the day were filled with righteous anger. Vipers, hypocrites, those who require impossibility in the name of God from their followers...the ones who talked big but lived small.[3] His estimation hearkens back to the scriptures in Isaiah:

> This people draw near Me with their mouth and honor Me with their lips but remove their hearts and minds far from Me, and their fear and reverence for Me are a commandment of men that is learned by repetition [without any thought as to the meaning].[4]

Words without actions speak volumes about the motive of the heart.

God hates injustice.

Christ wept over a city He loved that rejected Him.

⌐◝

In Matthew 18, Jesus is asked who is the greatest in the kingdom of heaven. Perhaps with a smile born of hidden humor, He pulls out the least likely example—a child. I think Jesus loved this golden opportunity to present the innocent beauty of children. Unless we can see the world through the eyes of children, we cannot be His. He spoke of angels from heaven that surround children. And in an in-your-face warning to anyone who might hurt an innocent child, Jesus equated inflicting pain on a child to pain inflicted on Him.

Children are open targets for pain. None of us have escaped childhood without some kind of wound. Children have no way of determining what is a toxic or honest response to life. And anger is part of the human experience. Children often have a pure response of rage at the outrageous, unjust garden they are born into.

Dealing with Anger

The human response to losses and injustices of all kinds may warrant anger. Anger is not the sin. It's what we do with anger that is the key. The apostle Paul writes, "When angry, do not sin; do not ever let your wrath (your exasperation, your fury or indignation) last until the sun goes down."[5]

This verse does *not* say, "Never be angry." To the contrary, Paul assumes we will feel anger, exasperation, fury, indignation. We will be angry. Now, to keep anger from taking over our spirits, we are encouraged not to sin with these natural feelings of loss. We must deal with them before we sleep, not allowing the anger to distill and grow even more bitter with the passage of time.

The following verse is less often quoted, but for me, it's the warning label on the side of the anger bottle: "Leave no [such] room or foothold for the devil [give no opportunity to him.]" Anger is nothing to be ashamed of. But don't let the enemy use it against you. Face the cause of anger, confront—in love and with all the calm you can muster—anyone, any situation, any cause of your frustration. If it's left inside your heart, it has the opportunity to make you physically and emotionally ill.

⌒

I studied, read, and sorted through all kinds of books, research, and statistics about depression while working on this project. Anger was addressed in all the writing I found on depression—and I believe it's an issue every honest person will admit to. The one element of recovery that was *not* included in secular research was the GET-OUT-OF-THE-ANGER-JAIL-FREE card offered to people of faith...

The cross of Jesus Christ.

The cross that so offends and staggers the world is the only place we ultimately have to take our deepest grievances, disappointments, and exhaustion.

Beverly, a beautiful lady of faith, is a counselor who lives in California and works with her husband through a ministry called Into His Rest Ministries. They are licensed therapists who try to speak healing: "for anxious souls, trust, for shattered lives, peace, and for the weary, rest." Many of their clients have been sexually abused or raped or are victims of incest—and are stuck in a myriad of depressive disorders. It was my good fortune to meet Beverly at a women's conference and go on a trip to New York and watch her in action.

She told me of a revelation God had given her to use with her patients. It's a radical, Scripture-based image she believes has set many of her suffering clients free from years of feelings of rage, injustice, and shame.

> I tell them to picture Jesus on the cross, and to place on Him every horrible thing that has ever happened to them....They need closure. They long for justice! When you look at Jesus on the cross, remember that He literally became every sin, every horror, every act of hideous injury perpetrated on an innocent child, every rape, every lie that has ever been or will be.
>
> Only from the lips of Jesus can you hear, "I am sorry."

From the cross of Christ we can find an answer to the source of our anger. God Himself is offering His deepest compassion. God Himself became all that went wrong, all we have done wrong, and He will say to our hearts, "I am sorry."

Justice from the cross, a glorious impossibility, offered freely to any of us willing to lay our burdens down and leave them there.

I am still learning to take the anger I feel about the losses in my life and look into the face of Christ to hear Him say, "I am sorry." He is sorry for the condition of the fallen world. He is sorry I never heard my earthly father tell me he loved me. He hates divorce and is sorry I was a single mom, sorry over the lies that tore at my heart and ministry.

From Anger…to Forgiveness

I'm also finding that God is never through with the broken places. The mending and healing continues.

What I was not able to hear from my daddy, I was given the chance to say to him over and over as he left for heaven. The only good aspect of Alzheimer's was that it allowed me to tell my father how much I loved him, countless times. I thanked him for teaching me about God and the words of Jesus. I thanked him for helping me raise my two children. I thanked him for showing me how a man can honor and love a woman, as he did my mom. And in the last few days, Daddy reached out to touch my face as a blind man might read the expression of a loved one. We sang "Jesus Loves Me" slowly in a whisper. We locked our eyes together during the painful moments he suffered at the end, and I know that daddy heard me…knew me…and the circle was complete. He gave me the gift of praying him into heaven. The last few minutes of his life I was the only one with him. And the last few seconds, my brother and I sang and rejoiced as Daddy was whole at last.

Depression set in for a time after I lost Daddy. But I keep reminding myself that in Christ, no one dies. He's gone on ahead of the rest of the family, but we'll catch up in time. As I reminded him so often, "Psalm 23 says you will go through the valley of the shadow of death, but you will not be afraid. It's a valley and a shadow, but your life is with Christ, Daddy. You will never die."

Anger takes one from anger of the loss to the forgiveness of the loss.

Something comes on the heels of anger issues, loss from diseases and the ugly demons of this upended world—and that is anger's cousin...forgiveness.

At first glance the two seem utterly estranged. But upon closer inspection, I find them joined at the hip.

When I was in the first stages of depression, Max Lucado suggested I might study and reflect on forgiveness. I rankled a bit at the implication. I had spoken forgiveness to the people who had hurt me in my life. I had dealt grace. I was not one to hold a grudge. Yet the urgency of finding relief brought me to a new examination of forgiveness.

⌒

What I discovered was humbling and healing.

On the night before Jesus was arrested, He shared the intimate, holy Last Supper with His apostles. He was full of love for His closest friends, and He spoke of how He had longed to celebrate this dinner with them. (Never cease to imagine Christ as the most compelling dinner companion of all time. What passion and charisma and honor and glory He must have embodied as God wrapped in human flesh!)

Jesus admitted to His disciples during this sacred time that one of them would betray and deliver Him to his enemies. Yet, even knowing of this painful betrayal, He fastened a servant's towel around his waist, took a basin of water, and with humility and tenderness washed their feet.[6] If I had been washing the dusty feet of my friends and was aware which one was about to have me killed, I think I might have skipped over that pair of sandals. Judas was treated exactly the same as all the others. Jesus did not embarrass him or turn to him in anger. Judas was included in the evening by a graciousness only Christ could have offered.

A Depth of Forgiveness Only God Understands

This story struck me deeply.

If Jesus could wash the feet of His betrayer, then I had no right to treat anyone with unforgiveness. What dusty feet might be under the table of my heart? What little pieces of unforgiveness might be eating away at my spirit?

During the ongoing inventory of those who have hurt me and who I have hurt, I've begun to pray blessing and forgiveness over all. Even myself.

So much grace has been lavished upon me. So many sins that litter my past and present, enough to cripple my back, are wiped away daily by a merciful God. The more I dip my soul into the pool of mercy, the more I long to be merciful.

When I begin to fall into the darkness of anger and unforgiveness, I force myself to pray good things for the person or situation that nips at my heels. It's not fun. It's downright uncomfortable. And I know that I cannot possibly begin to understand the depth of pain many have endured at the hands of their heartless tormentors.

Yet I know that God knows.

And even one inch of progress made toward forgiveness can push back the despair of depression.

> Forgiveness does not mean that what happened in the past does not matter. Rather, it is the effort made to give up the desire for revenge and punishment. Forgiveness can be a painful process. However, learning to forgive is about learning how to let go of hurts.
>
> To forgive ourselves means that we treat ourselves with compassion. We do not demand that we be perfect and not make mistakes.[7]

Forgiving ourselves allows us to accept our humanity and to ask God to fill up the places once filled with anger and resentment with more of the oil and wine of His grace.

Marilyn Ludolf writes of how forgiveness from the cross changed her heart:

> In my mind's eye, I could see Jesus hanging on the cross, suffering for me. He looked down at me with eyes full of love and concern. He asked me to forgive myself for all the times I had failed, for the hidden sins no one else knew about, for not measuring up to my goals, for the times I had failed myself, for the ways I had failed Him. And after I had brought all those hurts and pain to Him, it was as if He said, "It is finished!"[8]

On the cross, Christ finished what we find ourselves still struggling to complete.

∽

I was recently involved in a television taping in Israel. (That's another book in itself!) But one of the poignant discoveries for me was about the land God chose to give His people. It is an arid, varied, and beautiful terrain. It rains in Israel only four months out of the year. The rest of the time, the skies are clear blue during the day and full of stars at night. Yet without the rainfall, the crops fail and the people suffer. Our guide pointed out that God brought Israel into a land where they would be utterly dependent on His sufficiency for every necessity, even a glass of water.

Now for me, the Scriptures about water are more powerful than ever. Springs of water in a dry and thirsty land. The voice of God described by Ezekiel as the sound of rushing waters. Jesus saying to the brokenhearted Samaritan woman at Jacob's well, "I am the living water. Drink from me and you will never thirst again."[9]

From the side of Jesus on the cross, pierced by the sword, flowed blood mixed with water.

Perhaps streams of forgiveness were part of what Jesus refers to when He asks us to drink from the wine to remember what He came to do. He set captives free and broke the chains of death. His life gives life, and promises life forever.

When I commit myself to let go of anger, work through pain, and live forgiving others, I feel like I'm closer to flowing in the living water of Jesus Christ.

Healing commences.

Back up the ladder we move, a bit lighter now, letting go of the weight that brought on the fall.

Spiritually, physically, emotionally, keep climbing.

~

You cause my lamp to be lighted and to shine;
The Lord my God illumines my darkness.
For by You I can run through a troop,
And by my God I can leap over a wall.

FROM PSALM 18

The abundant wealth of the Dead Sea

shall be turned to you,

unto you shall the nations come

with their treasures.

~

FROM THE PROPHET ISAIAH

11

FASTEN YOUR SEAT BELTS—
THIS RIDE TURNS OVER

I am so grateful to you for coming along this far on a difficult but productive journey back up the ladder of your life again. We've looked through a lot of painful aspects of recovery, and I wanted to stop here for a fun tidbit of trivia and truth.

Depressive episodes work intensely to color our world with black and grey. For me, it felt like depression defined me and my future. But we serve a God who loves to turn the tables on defeat and who never gives up. The more I know Him, the more I adore Him, and the more I am stunned by His marvelous sense of humor.

Searching for a biblical reference about depression brought me to the sixtieth chapter of Isaiah—not a problem for me, as Isaiah is my favorite book. This passage began well:

> Arise [from the depression and prostration in which circumstances have kept you—rise to a new life]! Shine (be radiant with the glory of the Lord), for your light has come, and the glory of the Lord has risen upon you![1]

Terrific, Lord, I thought. *Yes! I want to encourage my depressed friends to know that You will cause them to rise up from their desolation and have a new life! This Scripture is a foreshadowing of the Messiah to come.*

Then I read on, following the passage as it moved on to describe how we shall "see and be radiant, and your heart shall thrill and tremble with joy [at the glorious deliverance] and be enlarged..."[2]

Okay, great. I'm there. This is good, Lord. We will be moved and thrilled in our heart by Your deliverance.

Suddenly the ride flipped over. Verse five was all about the abundance of the Dead Sea. *The Dead Sea? Lord, how can I use a scripture about depression recovery that lands me in the Dead Sea?*

Then I was thrilled, elated, and rejoicing when I read the research done on what was considered to be a lifeless body of water.

Prior to the twentieth century, scholars could only guess at what Isaiah referred to as the riches of the Dead Sea. Maybe he was a bit delusional from too much time spent prophesying to a devastated nation.

For ages, the Dead Sea represented a place of death and desolation. In 1935, though, its waters were found to contain important chemicals. Chemicals are fine—but how does this apply to rejoicing?

Still not impressed, I came upon the words of a scholar, G.T.B. Davis, from a book called *Rebuilding Palestine:*

> One is almost staggered by the computed wealth of the chemical salts in the Dead Sea. It is estimated that the potential value of the potash, bromine and other chemical salts of its water is...four times the wealth of the United States![3]

What Isaiah could not possibly have known, God gave to him as a prophecy of what Israel would inherit.

What looked like a dead sea—wasted, worthless, full of nothing but despair, was indeed laden with priceless treasures!

⤿

As we move into the final chapters of this book, I want to rejoice with you that what depression tries to steal away, God will redeem. He takes dead bodies of water and allows valuable, productive chemicals to be distilled from them.

And depression is so very much about chemicals out of whack, signals in the brain not connecting, genetic predispositions to varieties of the disease.

Yet in the hands of God, who is leading you and me to wade into what appear to be lifeless waters, we can find the richness of His salvation. We trust in Him. We find medical and emotional resources. We let go of unnecessary pain. We find the places in our hearts pressed into gems by a process the enemy hoped would destroy us.

In God's hands, even a dead sea can be a reservoir of teeming life.

∿

Sometimes the pilot of a ship can use a storm to make headway, instead of being wrecked by it.

BILLY SPRAGUE

Letter to a Grieving Heart

Now, with God's help
I shall become myself.

~

SØREN KIERKEGAARD

12

BRIDGE OVER CHAOS—1

Graham, my son, has a terrific way with words. He loves to laugh at me, especially when I'm way off base and the whole family can see it. Recently I told him I was speaking at a church event titled "Just Say No." The theme would be about rest and how to prioritize your life. Graham burst into laughter. "Mom, you are the poster child for doing this wrong! They ought to stand you up in a corner with a sign that says, 'Do not do what this woman does!'"

"Thanks for the vote of confidence, Graham," I replied, and then we both had to laugh at the irony of my speaking about slowing down and saying "no."

Nearly every pastor, counselor, or good friend I spend any length of time with offers to buy me the book *Boundaries*. I have copies of several books about setting healthy limitations, and I continue to struggle with their suggestions. It's become a running joke. Women I meet on the road, after following me around during a conference, will often smilingly mention *Boundaries*. I mean well, but my tendency is to take on too many things, spinning as many plates as possible at one time hoping none come crashing down.

Depression stopped me down for a good while and forced on me an opportunity to reevaluate what I expect from myself, how I approach each day, and how I can make much-needed changes. Easier said than done. Yet one of the blessings of depression is that I will spiral down off the ladder if I live in chaos.

Chaos for each of us is different, but each of us has our own brand.

For me, chaos is doing five projects at the same time, all the while trying to travel/speak/sing and write, attend every activity for my kids, keep up with every friend, and then slap on a negligee at night so my husband will see me as the woman of his dreams. It's completely unrealistic. So why do I attempt the impossible?

Partly because it's my nature to push hard.

Partly because I have bought into commercials on television with images of digitally enhanced, skinny, wrinkle-free women holding down jobs, and maintaining spotless homes, with newly washed clothes piled neatly in stacks smelling like spring flowers. The images finish off with slow-motion videos of these super-women gleefully throwing their children in the air as their handsome husbands flip a burger on their greaseless grill.

Partly because, as a woman of faith, I feel pressure to be all things to all people.

> Misinformation about the Bible's answers to these issues has led to much wrong teaching about boundaries. Not only that, but many clinical psychological symptoms, depression, anxiety disorders, eating disorders, addiction, impulsive disorders, guilt problems, shame issues, panic disorders, and marital and relational struggles, find their root in conflicts with boundaries.[1]

My tendency is to live in chaos. Coupled with a spongelike

personality and watching too much news, and knowing my tendency to respond on the dramatic side, I can easily bring on a chemical imbalance by living out of control. I'm learning to try to set walls around my life for protection. And enjoying discovering terrific reasons to be a bit selfish when it's called for.

The following ideas are for you to consider and personalize for your life and depression recovery.

1. Stress Management 101

Learn to say "no." We are taught by our culture and the Christian faith that we must serve, be hospitable, and give of ourselves. This is true, in perspective. What Jesus does not require is for us to neglect our own health—mental and physical—or our family in an effort to be on too many committees, run too many carpools, host too many Bible studies...the list goes on.

> Stress is probably the most common influence on our mood chemicals. Many depressions are triggered and maintained by stress, so it is worth spending a little time exploring the connection here. Stress can be related to...anxiety, irritability, fatigue and depression. Some people under stress are able to recognize it and back off from what is stressful to them. Others, however, are not able to escape from things that are stressful.[2]

Marriages could be spared so much agony if husbands and wives would truly cleave to each other first, and honor their parents by putting their new family first. Intrusive, demanding parents often leave you little choice other than to set barriers of protection around yourself and your family. It may feel horrible to say to your mother or father, "I have to do this with my family now. I love you and always will, but for the sake of my marriage, my children, and my home, I am going to say 'no' to your requests."

Saying "no" feels odd.

But after a while, it's very freeing to take control over your choices and say, "This is a place, activity, gift I believe I'm to be involved with"—and conversely, "This is something that will drain me, rob me of my ability to be all I can to my family and primary responsibilities." Someone else will fill in the gaps we leave.

> Made in the image of God, we were created to take responsibility for certain tasks. Part of taking responsibility, or ownership, is knowing what is our job, and what isn't. Workers who continually take on duties that aren't theirs will eventually burn out. It takes wisdom to know what we should be doing and what we shouldn't. We can't do everything.[3]

⌐

The age-old PKS—Preacher's Kid Syndrome—breaks my heart. How often have we seen children and spouses of pastors suffer because the church comes before the family? How can the church affect the culture around us with peace and goodwill when we are neglecting our own families in the name of serving God?

I pray we can find more ways to support our pastors with assistants and volunteers so that no one has to carry too much of the load. Pastors are not immune to marital problems and rebellious teenagers any more than their parishioners are. Yet the demands placed on them are staggering.

So many times I hear of a pastor committing suicide or being led into a relationship that promises the death of a marriage and a ministry. God gave us all different gifts so that, as a body, we can work together, not expecting to be "served" by a chosen few each Sunday who carry the responsibilities for everyone.

⌐

What is a boundary?

> Boundaries define us. They define what is me and
> what is not me. A boundary shows me where I end
> and someone else begins, leading me to a sense of
> ownership.[4]

Depressive seasons leave you feeling that you have no choices, no energy to say "no"—or "yes, for that matter. By evaluating who you are in realistic terms, then laying claim to your unique place in the world, you will find a vision of hope making its way onto your horizon.

> I've learned to say at times, with a smile but serious in tone, "No, I don't think I can do that right now. It wouldn't be good for me."

Depression recovery is a perfectly valid reason to say "no" to unrealistic requests so that you can keep getting stronger. I've learned to say at times, with a smile but serious in tone, "No, I don't think I can do that right now. It wouldn't be good for me."

A challenge for all of us is to evaluate who we allow to speak into our lives. It's not easy—but take inventory and pray about who you spend the most energy with, people you frequently listen to, talk on the phone with, go to movies and social events with—even sit beside at church. We all need healthy accountability with trusted friends and family when in a depression recovery. However, you may be shocked to realize some of the people closest to you can be a roadblock to your recovery.

Surprisingly, I have begun to accept that certain people in my life are pulling me down, and are not comforting to me. In the past I felt boxed in by a definition of their choosing—one I found negative and wanted to break free from. Slowly I began to limit my time with these people—some of them even lifelong relationships. It felt good to set healthy boundaries, to say, "'No, this is not who I am. I love you, but I am not who you tell me to be, even in subtle ways. How I spend my time and with whom is my choice. I won't be pressured or "guilted" into places that lessen my ability to be whole." I truly believe you will find yourself a bit gleeful inside when you learn to set serious boundaries. I'm with you on this; I'm still a novice at constructing new fences around my sanity. But fresh hope rushes in when I am free to open new gateways of my own choosing.

2. Victimization

Getting stuck as a victim of depression is truly the saddest of possibilities. At a Christmas event at which I was the guest speaker, the face of a lovely woman filled with anguish greeted me. It was a powerful night of "est fest"—"estrogen festival," as I love to call a gathering of women. Here were women encouraging each other, dressed to kill for the holidays, tables decorated each with a particular theme, a true celebration of girl-stuff…everyone oohing and ahhing!

Whenever I talk about the messy parts of my life, depression in particular, I know it may stir up many waters in the souls of hurting listeners. My desire is only to bring depression out of the closet and into the light. This particular night, one of depression's victims confronted me.

After several hours of sharing our hearts and our hope in the season celebrating the birth of Christ, this stunning, yet angry, woman approached me. I knew the night had been used by God, and that once again, through words and music and prayers, hearts had been moved closer to Him.

"You did nothing for me tonight!" she stated, eyes full of pain and longing. "You were supposed to give me hope! I've lost everything! I've lost my job, my home, my son, my purse, my life, my status! I was homecoming queen, and my family was wealthy! I came from somewhere, and now I have nothing!"

At first, I felt like I'd been slapped across the face. In all the times I've talked about the failures in my life, the times of despair, I've never painted a rosy picture of who I am or where I've been. It's all about what God has done with a broken woman. This was the first time I'd been attacked for what I see as being as transparent about my humanity as possible. What did I miss on this night when I felt the presence of God loving on all of us in the room?

I had been watching the lady's face as I spoke and sang. She had been sitting on the front row, squirming, now meeting my eyes, now turning abruptly away. There seemed to be no interaction between her and the other ladies at her table.

"I apologize to you with all of my heart," I said to her. Then for over an hour, as everyone but the staff left the building, she and I talked. I hugged her, I cried with her. I kept asking God to give me anything to say to help her.

"I came here tonight to find hope! And I'm leaving here without any!" she declared again. "I used to be someone! I was sought-after, and then my ex-husband took it all."

I continued to listen and attempt to hear her heart. "God will not leave you this way forever, " I assured her. "He is merciful, and I know He can do what I failed to do tonight. He will love you through this."

"Well," she demanded, "He had better show up soon. I've about had enough! I've been robbed six times, and had my car broken into. God took my oldest son, 23 years old—took him in a car crash! He was the only good thing left in my life, and now I have nothing!"

She was dressed to the nines, had on a fur coat, and sported a huge diamond ring. Slowly I began to see the bitterness in her eyes.

"Are you engaged now?" I asked hopefully.

She looked down. "Well, we aren't engaged. We're living together and he won't go to church with me. I don't know…he seems to love me."

Suddenly it all came together for me. She was unhappy with herself, disconnected from God, and stuck in a cycle of blaming God for everything that continued to go wrong in her life. She was a bona fide slave to depression.

Later I was told that she had been unhappy from the beginning of the night, even complaining to the gentlemen who helped park her car.

Repeatedly she explained the horror of her son's car crash, and in the same sentence would insist on telling me about her past social status, the money her family once had, the awards her dead son had won. I saw that she had yoked her heart to everything but the cross of Christ. Depression had declared victory over her life, and she was clinging to depression as her identity.

We offered to walk her to her car as she left, but she shook her head and made a comment about how she wasn't afraid, and was used to things going wrong. She could take care of herself.

Never have I met anyone so desperately in need of help. I suggested she might visit the church where I was speaking. They have a powerful counseling ministry and a heart of compassion for people. She didn't seem that interested in help. She was strangely comfortable being a victim.

One of the most tragic losses is someone who embraces the death of depression as a life sentence.

3. Be Careful Not to Isolate Yourself

Depression feels so unattractive, so deathly horrible, that the first tendency we have is to pull away from everyone. Our energy is sapped, our thinking is sad, our outlook bleak.

Yet one of the absolute worst ways to deal with depression is by retreating into ourselves. First of all, in a depressed state, we cannot be trusted to know how to take care of ourselves. Left alone, we will either undereat, or overeat, oversleep, or under-sleep; we will self-medicate, and we'll nurse false images about who we are.

> When a person rejects himself, he finds it difficult to enjoy other people. He tends to be supersensitive to others' attitudes toward his appearance, capabilities, parental background, or environment. Therefore he withdraws so as to avoid conflict and the unhappy feelings it creates. As he retreats, he muses increasingly upon his own needs, feelings, and thoughts. Since he doesn't like himself anyway, he becomes more unhappy.[5]

Of course, there is a fine line between avoiding isolation and trying to avoid depression by overinvolvement or manic activity. Depression recovery both requires quiet time to regroup, rest, and restore what's been depleted, and time to enter into the world again. Contrasts of good down time and invigorating time with friends will balance out life and give you back the energy to face each day.

When I was in the worst part of my depression, I began to have anxiety attacks about what normally wouldn't have caused me to blink an eye. I was afraid to go to the grocery store. I would avoid phone calls, make excuses for staying indoors with my shades drawn, not thinking clearly, imagining I could not cope with the necessary, easy tasks.

I wrote a piece called "Navel-Gazing." It was a guide to futility, written in the voice of Satan—along the lines of C.S. Lewis's, *The Screwtape Letters.* In my short experiment, I listed ten ways to focus on my pain and stay stuck in my depression. One of the ten was to avoid other people at all costs! Navel-gazing will most surely keep a depressed person focused on their misery.

Fighting against isolation, mustering all of my energy, I would force myself to go to the store, or drive to the post office or bank, and just go through the normal motions of taking care of life. Without fail, driving alone would lift my spirits. Getting out of the house, out into the light, out into a world, put my "navel" into perspective.

Life was going on. Now, did I want to get on with it or not? I had all the tools in place to recover. It was up to me to fight for my life.

↜

Early into my second marriage, though loved by Brent, the miracle in my life, I went into a serious depression. On the surface, there was no apparent reason for me to be depressed. We were madly in love, and my children were being treated with great affection and were happy. We moved to a beautiful farm outside of Franklin, Tennessee, and all of the changes were above and beyond my wildest expectations.

Yet I was depressed.

Below the surface, I was overloaded with changes and the unexpected unmet expectations in our new life. Brent is a recording engineer and producer. He's highly talented and in demand, and his hours can be long and arduous. My work involves an erratic schedule of recording, writing, and travel. Mix the two of us together, and you have no consistent or predictable family time.

We went through ten weeks of counseling during our engagement, and I thought we were prepared for the pitfalls and challenges. What I didn't factor in was reality. When the "picture" of what I thought our marriage would look like came up against the demands of moving, work, and less time together than when we were dating, I hit a wall of loss...and grief. I had to learn to fight again.

Brent wrote to me in a card, three months into our marriage,

> I spent all day looking at a picture of a beautiful,
> happy blonde and when things started to get rough at
> the studio today, just looking at you made me realize

all I have to be thankful for. Thank you for sharing
you and your kids with me, and if you know any way
I can put a smile on that blonde's face again, let me
know. Help me be the kind of husband God wants me
to be.

I responded to my patient husband out of my depression.

You deserve someone healthy and strong—like you—
who can dig into the green earth and beautiful long
days without giving out. I am so very weak. I guess
I'm just too weary now to be what you need.
Somehow God will work all this to good. I'm sorry
I'm not well enough to be happy. I want to be. My
body and emotions seem to betray me—my will is for
more—I am just so tired. And no one can walk the
road back but me. I want to walk it back.

It was my time to fight. To fight hard, and I did.

The depression was treated, and I grew stronger. It was my
choice not to pull back and isolate myself, but to share my most
private struggles with Brent while moving ahead, grateful for his
support.

⌒

One of the greatest friends in my life suffers with extreme
bouts of depression. He battled isolation for years. After a mirac-
ulous time of healing, he was blindsided by a horrific depressive
nosedive. He had turned into a person initiating and enjoying
gatherings of friends. Daily he had immersed himself in reading
the Bible. His work had never been more meaningful and effective. Suddenly, he was in the blackest hole. His medications had
been working well. He had been through a series of counseling
sessions that had unlocked much loss in his life. Why the setback?

He told his wife he was going to take a walk by himself and
think things through. When he returned, he looked in his wife's

worried face and said, "I clearly heard from God—you have to fight!" His spirit was being attacked by the only thing the enemy knew might bring him to his knees—depression. Yet he had enough of the Word of God in his soul to know that "greater is He that is in You than he that is in the world." It didn't mean, however, that he would not be asked to fight with all he had. Prayer and following the path of healing he understood brought a quick end to the latest battle.

Don't be surprised by setbacks along the way. It's part of the human struggle.

But a clear understanding of depression gives us the weapons to beat back the darkness.

We can choose life or death.

Keep on choosing life!

In order to live consistently in joy

people must set aside times

especially devoted to it.

~

MIKE MASON
Champagne for the Soul

13

BRIDGE OVER CHAOS—2

4. Sabbath Time

This is one of my pet peeves and favorite subjects to address. Down time! I fear it's because I'm an abysmal failure at making a place for consistent down time in my life. It's a goal, a dream I have of finding a way to "exhale" with God every day. Sabbath, resting time, is critical for depression recovery. This is God-isolation—the time when you can just be...and hear Him speak to your heart of how He loves you. It's time when your body and mind can refuel and face life refreshed. And how much we need it:

> The theology of progress forces us to act before we are ready. We speak before we know what to say. We respond before we feel the truth of what we know. In the process, we inadvertently create suffering, heaping imprecision upon inaccuracy, until we are all buried under a mountain of misperception.
>
> But Sabbath says, Be still. Stop. There is no rush to get to the end, because we are never finished. Take time to rest, and eat, and drink, and be refreshed...

> Listen to the sound the heart makes as it speaks the
> quiet truth of what is needed.[1]

Ette Hillesum, a young Dutch woman who survived the Nazi concentration camps, put it simply: "Ultimately, we have just one moral duty; to reclaim large areas of peace in ourselves."

The world demands more and more of us. The 24/7/365 mentality promises that our culture will put up few roadblocks. But it's up to each of us to make our own Sabbath time.

God commanded that the earth and His people take time for rest. It's one of the big ten commandments put on the back burner in our ever-more-enlightened world. After creating the world, God Himself rested on the seventh day. The God who says He does not sleep took a day off. Why? To set an example for us thickheaded humans who many times refuse to see a need to slow down until we have a breakdown.

⤳

When I am on the road, it's always invigorating, but it's tiring and an unrealistic experience compared to my life at home. People drive me to hotels, pay for my food, or take me to dinner. There are baskets of wonderful gifts, and I am focused only on the ministry I have to do with each group.

Then reality sets in. I call it "reentry." Back on the airplane, I try and prepare myself for lugging the luggage back to my car, driving home, and walking into a house looking pretty much like I left it. Now there are two men at home, my husband and my son, who rarely see a need to make a bed, or buy milk, or do any of the things "Mom" does when she's around.

Almost every reentry is bumpy for me. There is definite turbulence. I get irritated at the responsibility waiting—the bills to pay, the e-mails to answer, the laundry piled high, and the grocery trips to make. But I do much better with reentry if I decide to reward myself with some Sabbath time.

I've been working, so I will take a day off and rest. No matter what day it is, I call it my Sabbath day.

I will purposefully let the laundry wait one more day, order in pizza, and close my door and be alone with God. I might actually take a nap…the ultimate treat.

Sabbath rest is not politically correct. We are supposed to run full steam ahead—but to what end? I find it fascinating that in an age that has produced more appliances and gadgets to make life easier, I hear from more burned-out, worn-out people than ever before. It seems the more we have, the more we take on.

Worry is tied up in the Sabbath question. If we take time off, will we be replaced in the workplace by someone younger and more assertive? If we lose work, we'll lose income—and how will we pay for school and cars and groceries and insurance? Won't the house of cards come tumbling down?

But there's no way to give too much credit to the importance of one day of rest. Why else would the Creator of our bodies command that we recharge our batteries spiritually, emotionally, and physically?

The Lord God commanded that even the land of Israel be allowed to rest every seven years. Animals, land, and yes, we humans do require time off.

I feel so passionately about this issue because I've been taught by my own body and mind breaking down that when I do not get enough time away—time with God, time to do just plain nothing—I will come apart at the seams.

So take a bubble bath. Walk through a park; drive to a small town and eat lunch at a little diner. Sit outside and watch the stars. Just every so often, let yourself be—as you were made for in the Garden—in the very undemanding presence of God.

Mother Teresa once said, "God is the friend of silence."

Arsenius, one of the early Christian Desert Fathers, said, "I have often repented of having spoken, but never of having kept silent."[2]

Take off your shoes, take off your "have to's" and "should have's," and every so often, as often as you can, put them on a shelf far away.

The Lord will indeed lead you beside still waters, and there you may just find He will restore your soul.

5. Self-Image, Not Self-Esteem

The older I get, the less patience I have with what is fed to me and my family through, as my daddy wisely called it, the "boob tube." He meant the "idiot" tube, but unfortunately it has now morphed into a place where the human anatomy shows up in living color on reality shows abounding.

In one of my less stellar attempts at diplomacy, I erupted during the pre-telecast of an awards show at our house. Suddenly I was overwhelmed with the idolatry in front of me. People in the stands had waited all day to catch a glimpse of other people—movie stars and musicians. The first group of people were screaming like mad for the second group of people, who walked down a red carpet, cameras flashing to take their pictures, while the people in the stands hoped the others might glance their way.

People, when it all boils down, are all just people. We all wake up in the morning facing our humanity and what we will do with the choices before us.

Well, the people on the red carpet were waxed, botoxed, lifted, and draped in all manner of jewels and gowns only a trainer could have prepared them for. They were already being treated as idols and were about to go into a room where they would be awarded golden statues for their work.

My kids were eating it up.

I nearly threw up.

I was kindly asked to go into another room as I was spoiling the family's fun. They were not so serious about the awards and just wanted to see the idols receive their idolatry in peace.

↜

I cannot help but see that many subtle—and not-so-subtle—messages come at us about who we are "supposed to be" through the media, magazines, and billboards.

An astute pastor addressed his congregation recently about the slick, treacherous infiltration of pornography. "Our wives will never live up to the women presented on these Web sites and on television. They simply cannot compete, nor should they have to!"

Depression may occur for you after someone you love rejects you, or you have been dealing with the pain of family abuse or the loss of a job or financial ruin...I don't know what may have triggered your fall.

It's vitally important for you to begin to see yourself as a child of God the King—and to treat yourself with the same R-E-S-P-E-C-T that you would show anyone you love. The way you view yourself and life will affect your depression recovery.

I love this quote from Linda Dillow's book *Calm My Anxious Heart:*

> Two women looked through prison bars,
> One saw mud, another saw stars.

When depressed, I tend to see mud. But I long to raise my eyes to the vista of the stars.

> Each of us has a choice about how we look at life: We can focus on the mud or lift our eyes and see the stars. Every woman has circumstances that appear to be prison bars. God wants you and me to learn to be content in our circumstances, not when they improve.[3]

Learn to filter out what you expose yourself to, both in the news and from the media. Treat your psyche as a treasured part of your being. What goes into the eyes, comes out of the heart. So we can play a huge role in the movies, books, and people we allow into our view.

And do not be afraid to love and accept yourself just as God made you.

How many times we have heard, "You are what you think you are." Sounds instinctive, and simple enough. But this phrase is packed with implications. I will be what I see myself to be. If I see myself as a failure and my depression as having control over me, then I will live up to those expectations. If, however, I see myself as a child of God, with opportunities to fight any disease—not defined by my weak moments but accepted and loved through them—I will live accordingly. If I allow other people to tell me who I am, then I run the risk of trying to be all things to please everyone simultaneously. Perhaps a parent or spouse or friend has repeatedly offered negative input about me. Who do I allow to define my self-image? The One who made me, or other flawed human beings around me?

Jesus commanded us to love our neighbor as we love ourselves. There's not much loving going on anywhere until we accept our limitations and our depressive tendencies, and trust that God accepts us and delights over us no matter what we think we should be.

> A mature person has freedom not only to laugh and to cry if the occasion warrants, but also to respond emotionally to those around him. His joy is not dependent upon people or circumstances, but radiates from within.[4]

As you reprogram the chip in your brain that tells you who you are and how you are loved, be sure to program in a space that allows yourself a wide range of feelings. It's how you are wired. Depression exposes old emotions that have been shut down. They surface in abundance and demand to be reckoned with. This is a healthy process. Your body and mind are raising a red flag for help.

Believe me, the faucet of tears will flow less and less as you allow yourself to heal. Laughter and joy and anger and sorrow weave in and out of every human heart. When you're depressed they may be out of kilter for a time, but with proper treatment you will find your balance once more. Attempts to deny feelings will only stymie the healing process. Give yourself a break and allow some volcanoes to erupt. In safety, with God's guidance through counselors and doctors, you can move ahead—as Paul says, "Forgetting what lies behind and straining forward to what lies ahead, I press on toward the goal to win the…prize to which God in Jesus Christ is calling us upward."[5]

Up the ladder!

As you recover, examine the tapes you've played in your head about who you are. Throw out the old tapes that are toxic, including lies from family, even from close friends—lies you have repeated to yourself so often that they threaten to become truth. God will *never* condemn you or put you down! Those voices are not from the heart of your Father. Put in new information to displace the lies:

- God sings over you with delight.[6]

- God has a plan and a future for you filled with hope.[7] This promise was given to Israel in the midst of their captivity. As depression has been your captor, receive the unfailing blessing of God into your heart.

- Psalm 139 explains how God knew everything about you—every little detail as you were being formed in your mother's womb. He knew the hairs of your head, the days of your life—and nothing about your journey is unbearable or too dark for His eyes. No matter what's happened—if you have attempted suicide, found yourself among those who cut themselves to make sure they are alive, been through abortion, rape, incest, divorce, addiction—the Word of God says you are "fearfully and wonderfully made."

- Begin to keep a journal if you can. Write down the simple ways God speaks hope to you in your recovery. Write the vision, as Habbakuk says in chapter 2—the vision of who God says you are. Begin the process of believing His resume about you, over and above your own.

⤿

[Inasmuch as we] refute arguments and theories and reasonings and every proud and lofty thing that sets itself up against the [true] knowledge of God; and we lead every thought and purpose away captive into the obedience of Christ (the Messiah, the Anointed One).[8]

How many times I've said to people who fall weeping on me at events, grasping for hope, "Jesus is crazy about you! He died for you!"

Over and again I will hear in response, "I don't feel the love! How can I make it without feeling it?"

⤿

The light will always defeat the dark. We have *His* word on that.

⤿

And I remember so well that when I was in the agony of my clinical depression the truths of the Gospel rang hollow. Intellectually I knew Jesus died for me, and that I must matter somehow in the scheme of things. But I didn't feel anything but a sense of death.

Feelings can *lie.*

Feelings of negative self-image are not to be trusted when you are climbing the ladder back up into life again. (Scotty Smith, pastor at Christ Community Church in Franklin, Tennessee, prefers the term *self-image* to *self-esteem* because we were created in the image of God, and we cannot be trusted to esteem ourselves apart from His care.)

Trust in God and in His promises whether you feel the sun shining on your face or the darkness closing in. The light will always defeat the dark. We have *His* word on that.

> To be grateful for an unanswered prayer, to give thanks in a state of interior desolation, to trust in the love of God in the face of the marvels, cruel circumstances, obscenities and commonplaces of life is to whisper a doxology in darkness.[9]

6. Guilt and Shame

There's no getting around the sense of failure attached to a depressive episode. It could be the ugliest aspect of the disease.

The word *shame* comes from the Indo-European root *skam,* meaning "to hide." Adam and Eve hid from God after disobeying His command that they not eat from the tree of good and evil.[10] Shameful feelings make us want to hide from others we feel we have failed, or who see us as failures.

Guilt and shame arise from depression when we believe we "ought" to be fine. Please do not let these feelings keep you from seeking help in all the areas we've looked at in this book.

We would not shame someone who is physically ill. We would do all we could to pray for them and speak hope to them, and to get medical attention as soon as possible. And there's no shame in falling ill emotionally, especially when losses in life bring on more than we can bear.

In the garden of Gethsemane, Jesus sweat great drops of blood while praying to God over the painful crucifixion he faced. In other words, Jesus suffered a medical condition induced by extreme stress. "If this cup can pass from me," Jesus asked. "If there is any other way…" and the Word made flesh agonized over the state of the world.

Brennan Manning writes of a dear friend's experience while he was praying over the passage in John 1:

> "The Word was made flesh, and he lived among us…"
> In the bright darkness of faith, he heard Jesus say, "Yes, the Word was made flesh. I chose to enter your broken world and limp through life with you."[11]

If Jesus could suffer extreme stress without shame, then so can we. Depression does not imply a lack of faith. It's a condition of the heart and body brought on by living in a broken world.

Perhaps a sinful area in your life has sparked a depressive episode. Here again, confession is healing for the soul. The Holy Spirit of God is the gift Christ gave us that gently prods each of us to come clean about hidden sin. One of the authors I read commented that he had no reason for his clinical depression. He went on to describe his life as full of worldwide travel and a bisexual freedom he enjoyed. I was immediately struck with the sin in his sexual life, and how out of synch this man was with who God made him to be. No wonder years of living out of a suitcase, partying, and sleeping with men and women left him to wake one day with a dark sense of gloom.

For those of us who can drink deeply from the wells of grace, there is no condemnation in Christ Jesus. Take inventory of your inner life, and break free from anything that blocks your vision from seeing yourself as a beloved child of God.

So much was suffered by Jesus, a man of sorrows and acquainted with grief, so that you and I don't have to be ashamed of disease. Our diseases were healed by the wounds of Jesus on the cross. Physical and mental disease was nailed down with Him. But guilt and shame fuel the fires of low self-image, hold hostage the beauty of hope, and promote victimization.

There are times when I have a small private ceremony.

On small pieces of paper, I write down false beliefs about myself, sins I need to confess, and lies from my past, and then I pray that God will allow me to leave them at the foot of the cross. Then I light a candle beside me. After the prayer, I tear up the pieces of paper, blow out the candle, and throw them away. It's even more fun when I'm in front of a fireplace and can watch them burn. On occasion, I and others have taken our pieces of paper and literally left them in a box at the foot of a cross.

Whatever it takes, send unmerited guilt and shame packing.

Joy waits in the wings!

7. Ageless Hope

Joy isn't just for the young and middle-aged. The joy of the Lord is an ageless, timeless gift. Many beloved elderly people among us suffer from depression in silence. Perhaps the death of a spouse leads them a place of wondering if life offers any reason to push through. Perhaps it's a loss of family, friends, job, and the ability to navigate in their aging earth-suit with the same ease as in earlier times.

Recent research is showing that depression puts many elderly people at risk of suicide. For years the medical field did not recognize how all people of all ages respond to wise treatment. One recent study included 1800 people 60 and older who had symptoms of a major depressive episode. Most of these former thriving patients had lost interest in activities and felt a cloud of uselessness over their lives. The more depressed the person became, the more likely they were to enter a nursing facility, at times prematurely.[12]

Families are usually the first to notice when an elderly member stops paying bills and preparing meals, and resists help with medication or therapy. Please do not take lightly the warning signs that may indicate depression with seniors: immense trouble sleeping, and "checking out" from activities that formerly gave them joy.

A friend of mine who works as a hospice nurse with the elderly offered me a simple way she uses to engage older people who are depressed. She looks for a key ingredient to their life that can be reintroduced in a creative manner. For example, my father struggled with depression during various phases of his Alzheimer's disease. He knew something was going terribly wrong and was unable to stop the disease from robbing him of his life. When Daddy was healthy, he loved to read. He devoured books and thrived on increasing knowledge. (He read blueprints of computers for fun!) When he began to appear despondent, we took him anything that required using numbers to operate. I first noticed his interest in my cell phone. He would reach for it and take it from me, and begin to play with the key pad. After that, we gave him calculators, puzzles, and a cell phone that wouldn't dial out but gave him great delight.

Daddy also had books he would look at and read, full of pictures and text—adult books treating him as an adult—albeit one trapped in a mind that was deteriorating. He read, then reread them, speaking sentences out loud until he could no longer speak.

꙳

Psalm 71 gives voice to the elderly who love the Lord and need to know no matter what our physical age, God's love and care for will never change:

> Lord, you are my hope. Lord, I have trusted you since I was young. I have depended on You since I was born; you helped me even on the day of my birth. I will always praise you...

> Even though I am old and gray, do not leave me, God. I will tell the children about your power; I will tell those who live after me about your might...

I will praise you with the harp. I will trust you, my God.

Every life is sacred, down to the last breath taken this side of God's presence. In Revelation, harps are mentioned as being played by the saints—not little angelic babes floating in the by-and-by, but those who loved God and trusted in Christ for their future. Perhaps the elderly are readying themselves to be harpists praising their Father. Let us not lose sight of every bit of wisdom and joy they have to share with the world, and offer to them every ounce of grace and restoration if they fall into depression.

~

Sometimes joy is what seeps through the cracks when our hearts are breaking. . . When joy's heart breaks, it's because joy feels free and safe enough to embrace everything, even the feeling of falling to pieces.

MIKE MASON

Champagne for the Soul

The miracle of joy is this: it can happen

when there is no apparent reason for it.

Circumstances may call for despair. Yet, something

different rouses itself inside us . . . We remember God.

We remember He is love. We remember He is near.

~

RUTH SENTER
For A Woman's Heart

14

Resurrected Heart

'm a pushover for the underdog. Give me a story where the least likely character wins, and tear-stained Kleenexes go flying.

In the movie *Miss Firecracker*, I find myself utterly drawn to the character of Carnelle. She is the youngest child in a family of losers. Her cousin, a classic middle child, roams haplessly from sleeping in railroad cars to part-time jobs disposing of dead animals. He is a simple man, but his heart is good, and his inherent charm serves to keep him above water.

The oldest cousin is the only success of the three by the world's standards. She is a tall beauty who manipulates and controls each situation to her own advantage, no matter what the cost—even to her closest relatives. She marries a wealthy man from Memphis, who sends her dozens of roses to keep her happy. A former beauty queen, she was once the winner of the Independence Day pageant. In the town parade she wore a legendary red gown, a crown on her long, brunette hair...

Carnelle dreams of winning the crown for herself one day, like the older cousin she reveres. She practices tap-dance routines lying on the floor of their worn-down home, pounding away on the cabinet doors in the kitchen.

Carnelle is an utterly enchanting loser. She dyes her hair bright red and auditions for the county beauty pageant, surrounded by a handful of misfit characters who share her excitement. Carnelle's stellar cousin is in town for the event, and with her other ragtag cousin and a handful of friends, watches events unfold from the sidelines.

Carnelle begs her beautiful cousin to borrow the magical red gown, but alas, it hasn't been packed. So Carnelle comes up with her own makeshift pageant dress and walks proudly out onto the stage. During the talent competition, she is publicly ridiculed by those in the audience who know of her less-than-honorable life offstage. In a pageant with only five contestants, she finishes last.

To complete her humiliation, she returns home to find the coveted red gown hidden in her cousin's luggage. It was there all along. Evidently, the winner's circle in the family was guarded with meticulous, "bless your heart" care.

Later, Carnelle reveals her pain to one of her best friends, Max Sam, a carnival worker.

"I just don't know what you can reasonably hope for in this life," she says through her tears.

Max inhales from his cigarette, and after an agonizing cough, he turns to Carnelle and smiles. "There's always eternal grace."

Eternal grace.

Grace shows up for Carnelle when she realizes that she has a lot to offer the world. She takes her eyes off her oldest cousin, awakening to the fact she has lived her life in the shadow of a lie. The movie ends with Carnelle racing to the top of the lighthouse in town, watching the fireworks going off for the Independence Day celebration. She may have lost the beauty pageant, but she has won a greater prize in finding herself.

She is smiling. She has discovered grace.

Finding Grace...Finding God

Graham was a young boy in elementary school when he explained grace to me with profound understanding: "Grace is like climbing a ladder, Mom. You go up a few steps, then you fall back down a few. You go up a little more and try harder, then maybe fall again. But no matter where you are on the ladder, Jesus is at the top. He will always reach down and pull you all the way up."

My friend, there is joy in knowing that no matter where we are on our ladder back out of depression, we can count on the certainty of God's eternal grace. I move up a few steps and down a few from time to time, but I keep looking up—and at the top of the ladder there is the face of Christ, urging me on, His hands stretched down to take mine.

Depression recovery is like waking from a long, restless sleep, filled with dreams of torment, picture shows of failures, tears wetting the pillow. When we find ourselves moving up the ladder again, the simplest moments in life are transformed into holy miracles by God's grace.

Do not be afraid of what you have suffered, or that you may fall again into an even darker space. You now have the knowledge of what this disease can bring and how to fight for your life in a bold, straightforward way. My great-aunt Helen spoke about the great gift of understanding depression. She said that after her initial battles with the disease, the insight she gained was immeasurably valuable. Knowledge is a form of insurance. "There were a few grey days that lay ahead, but never again the blackness." Her words comfort me.

Questions about why I suffered depression, why it is part of my chemical makeup, why God would allow this disease to hurt so many people, prove pointless. I've learned to accept the unanswerable questions and know that God uses everything for my good if I take it to Him. His ways are not mine. I do believe God's love is the one constant I can put my full weight upon. He never intended disease to be a part of the human equation. And through the magnificent defeat accomplished by Jesus on the cross, all sickness has been redeemed.

> "All too frequently we tend...to see our trials and temptations...as isolated nightmares. God, however, sees them from a different perspective. They are important and connected punctuation marks in the biography of grace. He is writing in our lives. They give formation, direction, and character to our lives. They are all part of the tapestry He is weaving in history."[1]

You have been through a season that stands as an exclamation mark of God's grace in the history of your life. In His hands, nothing is ever wasted. The time spent in the wilderness has brought you closer to Him, and it will fill you with a compassion to carry the torch of hope to others who may suffer as you have.

> To "walk in the light" means that everything that is of the darkness actually drives me closer to the center of light.[2]

I'd like to share the perspective of a friend with you. Let's call her Carla—her story can be attributed only to an unexplainable exclamation point of God's grace in her life.

Carla was married to the man she'd loved since she was 16 years old. After two miscarriages, she was finally the mother of a young son when she discovered the horrible news that her husband was having an affair. He promised to stop the relationship, but Carla began to spiral down into thoughts of suicide.

Several times she thought of driving through a barricade near the university where she was taking night classes. Only the eyes of her young son kept her alive.

Finally her pain was so intense that she could think only of dying. She dropped off her son at her mother's house, her purse full of sleeping pills, and drove to a motel.

She told no one where she would be, not even her mother.

Filled with complete and utter despair and hopelessness, Carla lay across the hotel bed and took out the pills. In her own words,

> I thought about how much I just wanted to take them and go to sleep and not have to think, not have to feel, not have to hurt again. I was so close to doing it...just going to sleep forever, when the phone rang. No one knew where I was!
>
> I picked up the phone and heard someone say, "Carla?"
>
> I answered, "Yes?"
>
> She said, "This is Nancy....(a close friend of mine from college that I hadn't seen or heard from in many years). The Lord told me to call this number and ask you what you were doing..."
>
> Stunned, I told her everything that had been going on.
>
> "Call your mom and let her know you are okay. And call your husband and let him know where you are so he can come and get you."
>
> It was literally a wake-up call to me, and definitely stopped me from taking a way out that I had been considering for some time.

Even knowing a God who works mysteriously, Carla was shocked when she later contacted Nancy about the phone call. Nancy had absolutely no memory of making it. She said, "Carla, it wasn't me. Perhaps the Lord intervened and had an angel call you, using my name and voice, knowing that you would receive my advice."

Carla and her husband began to rebuild their lives.

She admits to having other falls from her ladder, but the Lord's promises kept coming back to her. One night she stood in their backyard, in a drenching rain and cried out to God for help. Carla admits that it's the only time she has ever felt the voice of God speaking to her: *Carla, if you remain faithful to Me, and trust Me, then I will pour showers of blessings over you and yours even as this rain is soaking you now.*

She wrote a prayer in her Bible that God would remind her of His faithful promises when times get rough.

"And He has!" Carla smiled as she told me. "My favorite verse has been Isaiah 41:10—'Do not fear, for I am with you; do not anxiously look about you, for I am your God. I will strengthen you, surely I will help you, surely I will uphold you with My righteous right hand.' Bonnie, God is a God of restoration. He has restored us to a place of trust again. He has changed my heart and has literally saved me. It's not always been easy. But God has always been there...and I know he always will be."

~

For Carnelle, for my friend Carla, for you and me, life this side of heaven—dealing with depression and finding out who we are—is not a walk in the garden we were created for. Yet depression can lead us into a private, tender interaction with the Lord. Depression sheds new light into dark corners. It puts the ladder of our lives in the spotlight of mercy.

Luci Freed comments, "Because of the overpowering and oppressive nature of depression, some people believe that it is somehow their lot in life. Not true—you can move through, not surrender to it."[3]

I feel intimately connected to any of you who have moved through this book with me. We share a heart bond, a mutual victory in climbing out of the darkness of depression and back into life again. I pray for you that joy will begin to wash into your thoughts and restore your broken places.

A New Kind of Joy

As I began to recover, joy was the sweetest nectar that would drip, drip, drip into my soul. Joy is our inheritance from God.

There's a deep-down-to-my-bones joy in knowing who I am, and knowing that God has allowed me to overcome my depression. Joy isn't always jumping up and down with a feeling of overwhelming delight. Joy has a richer meaning now.

> Joy is living unafraid...Joy is sharing my hope with you!

There is sacred joy in the very act of waking up in the morning and holding onto hope. Joy is knowing I can control depression and that it does not have the power to ruin my life.

Joy is medication that keeps my body stabilized, doctors who are there to help, friends who hold me accountable, and gratitude for living in a time in history where depression can be treated.

Joy is the faces of my family and friends, and walking out on a clear night and seeing the miracle of a million stars.

Joy is taking my dear friend Janice out to lunch after she's visited her oncologist at the hospital. She's fighting against cancer—another horrific disease. And I have the rare joy of fighting with her.

Joy is resting, making myself plan down time, watching my children grow into adulthood, and delighting in the love of my Brent. Joy is learning to ride the horses my husband adores, even mucking out their stalls, and thanking God that He created such beautiful animals.

Joy is living unafraid.

"Joy is like a muscle, and the more you exercise it, the stronger it grows."[4]

Joy is sharing my hope with you!

I'm finishing this book on the first day of a new year. There was a time when January 1 caused me fear, dread, and tears. Now I can say I look forward to the new year because I know my Redeemer lives and stands with me in this wounded garden, preparing me to face one day at a time, and promising never to leave me without the hope of the garden to come.

Now go in the name of Jesus as your muscle of joy gets stronger, and help others to find their way out of the darkness.

> Thou Son of the Most High, Prince of Peace, be born again into our world. Wherever there is war in this world, wherever there is pain, whenever there is loneliness, wherever there is hope, come, thou long-expected one, with healing in thy wings.
>
> Wherever there is boredom, wherever there is fear of failure, wherever there is temptation too strong to resist, wherever there is bitterness of heart, come thou blessed one, with healing in thy wings.
>
> Saviour, be born in each of us who raises his face to thy face, not knowing full who he is or who thou art, knowing only that thy love is beyond his knowing, and that no other has the power to make him whole. Come, Lord Jesus, to each who longs for thee even tho he has forgotten thy name. Come quickly.[5]

Yes, Jesus, come quickly into each place we need Your mercy and grace.

Don't Be Afraid!

On the beaches of Florida, I have met God in more ways than I can count. Jesus has come quickly indeed into my life on several occasions where I raised an angry fist at the sky and struggled to keep my heart afloat.

Recently, I was not to be disappointed. God once more surprised me with His astounding presence and power, revealed in the activity on a white, sandy shore. Children ran to chase the waves as they lapped at their feet, as only children can do. They are able to see "delight" in creation without inhibition. Their arms and legs nearly come out of their sockets as they shout and laugh and run with sheer astonishment at the wonder of a vast ocean of green and blue, powerful in its ferocity and beauty. The mystery of God crashes with holy musical tones at every crescendo of waves emptied onto the sand.

I watched as seagulls dove into the water for food, and my own soul praised God for His creation, which sings of His glory.

Suddenly, two young women captured my attention. A sandbar waited for them several yards from the shoreline. One of the two had already made her way to the sandbar and back. She was insistent that her friend experience the same joy. But her friend was afraid of the waves, of the unknown power of the water.

"Don't be afraid! It's amazing!" the first cried out.

"I want to...it's just so cold!" her friend replied.

"Go ahead! Go into the water! Do you want me to go with you? I'm here!"

Enthralled by the invitation from one friend to another to dive into the glory of God's creation, I stood crying with happiness as I observed this unexpected, sacred event.

Inside my mind I joined in—*Yes, dive in, discover the water is good! It is the astounding goodness of a merciful God! Drink in the refreshment to your body and soul! Don't be afraid...You are not alone!*

The two friends were soon together on the sandbar, delighting in the sun and ocean waves and all God's creation has to offer. The courage of one friend who braved the waters gave hope to her friend to discover the joy of making her way to the new shore.

⌇

Jesus, the bread of life, is the water that fills our brokenness. The Holy One of God who reclaims us over and over again from despair and depression is the One I offer to you. As your friend, I pray this book will call out to you, "Don't be afraid. Do you want someone to join you in this adventure of life? The water is fine! It's great! There is hope! New shores are waiting. We are bonded in this quest together."

Go, my friends, out of the darkness, with healing in your heart, with joy in your spirit, with the light of hope on the horizon. Go, and do not miss one moment of your precious, beloved life!

~

"One Storm"

. . . and that one storm
it almost dragged me under
beneath the waves into the murky sea . . .

and that one storm
it only made me stronger
for it was there Your mercy carried me

and though I know
the storms of life may shake me
they will never overtake me

You're with me in the deep.

TRAVIS COTTRELL
AND MICHAEL MELLETT
from "The Deep," 2002[6]

RECOMMENDED READING

How to Win over Depression, Tim LaHaye
Reaching for the Invisible God, Philip Yancey
Overcoming Depression, Paul Gilbert
Noonday Demon, Andrew Solomon
Darkness Visible, William Styron
Calm My Anxious Heart, Linda Dillow
Sabbath, Wayne Muller
The Ragamuffin Gospel, Brennan Manning
A Season to Heal, Luci Freed
Happiness Is a Choice, Frank Minirth and Paul Meier
Boundaries, Henry Cloud and John Townsend
Telling the Truth, Frederick Buechner
Champagne for the Soul, Mike Mason
Telling Yourself the Truth, William Backus and Marie Chapian
The Freedom from Depression Workbook, Les Carter and Frank Minirth
Mercy for Eating Disorders, Nancy Alcorn
Ruthless Trust, Brennan Manning
The Word of God, the Psalms in particular

Recommended Resources for Recovery

In addition to contacting your pastor, doctor, and trusted friends and family, listen to music that will soothe your spirit. Music can play a vital part in stress reduction and relaxation. Remember as well that any exercise helps your body fight depression. Also, pay careful attention to what sort of images you expose yourself to via television, news, or movies. Treat yourself like fine china during recovery and watch for places that bring you strength.

Here are other resources to check into along the way.

1-800-SUICIDE

1-800-784-2433. Will connect you to the certified crisis center nearest you.
www.hopeline.com

Adolescent Suicide Hotline

1-800-621-4000

American Association of Christian Therapists (AACT)

aactonlinetx.tripod.com

Anxiety Disorders

11900 Parklawn Dr., Suite 100, Rockville, MD 20852
301-231-9350
www.adaa.org

Bipolar Depression Information

www.leverageTeamllc.com

Focus on the Family Crisis Hotline

1-800-A-FAMILY (1-800-232-6459)

Freedom from Fear

308 Seaview Ave., Staten Island, NY 10305
718-351-1717
www.freedomfromfear.org

Light Deprivation Resources

Balanced-spectrum floor lamp
1-800-811-8151
www.balancedspectrum.com

Medical Information—general

National Center for PTSD, Executive Division
VA Medical Center (116D), White River Junction, VT 05009
802-296-51320
www.ncptsd.org

Mental Health Questions—general

www.Godtest.com

National Christian Counselors Association (NCCA)

www.ncca.org

National Mental Health Association (NMHA)

1021 Prince Street, Alexandria, VA 22314
703-684-5968
www.nmha.org

Outreach for Hope National Links

www.nacronline.com

Suicide Hotlines

suicidehotlines.com

Teen Suicide Hotline

1-800-949-0059

NOTES

Chapter 1—A Garden Lost, a Garden Found

1. Brennan Manning, *The Ragamuffin Gospel* (Sisters, OR: Multnomah, 2000), p. 24.
2. Genesis 2:16-17.

Chapter 3—Down the Rabbit's Hole

1. Renée Coates Scheidt, *Songs of the Night: Singing Sorrow's Songs Through the Darkness of Grief* (Friendswood, TX: Baxter Press, 2000), p. 116.

Chapter 4—Name This Disease

1. Proverbs 2:3-5.
2. Richard O'Conner, *Undoing Depression* (New York: Berkley Books, 1999), p. 8.
3. Robert Short, *The Gospel According to Peanuts* (Louisville, KY: Westminster John Knox Press, 1965), p. 80.
4. Paul Gilbert, *Overcoming Depression* (New York: Oxford University Press, Inc., 2001), pp. 3, 13.
5. Job 23:8-9 NCV.
6. WebMDHealth, http://my.webmd.com/content/article/62/71501?z=3074_00000_16 63_00_02.
7. William Styron, *Darkness Visible* (New York: Vintage Press, 1992).
8. Gilbert.
9. Andrew Solomon, *The Noonday Demon* (New York: Simon & Schuster, 2002), p. 25.
10. O'Conner.
11. Les Carter and Frank Minirth, *The Freedom from Depression Workbook* (Nashville, TN: Thomas Nelson Publishers, 1995), p. 4.
12. Philip Yancey, *Disappointment with God* (Grand Rapids, MI: Zondervan, 1997), p. 183.

Chapter 5—The Cry of the Wounded

1. Frederick Buechner, *Whistling in the Dark* (New York: HarperSanFrancisco, 1993), p. 117.
2. John Eldredge, *Waking the Dead* (Nashville, TN: Thomas Nelson Publishers, 2003).
3. Luke 1:13 NCV.

Chapter 6—Shades of Black

1. C.A. Patrides, ed., "Herbert," *The English Poems of George Herbert* (Totown, NJ: Rowman & Littlefield, 1974), p. 159.

2. Ruth 1:20-21, brackets in original.

3. Ecclesiastes 4:1-2 NCV.

4. Jonah 2:2 NCV.

5. Jonah 4:2-3 NCV.

6. Job 19:7-10 NCV.

7. 1 Samuel 1:15-16 NCV.

8. Mark 14:34,36 NCV.

9. Mark 15:34 NCV.

10. As quoted in Richard O'Conner, *Undoing Depressions* (New York: Berkley Books, 1999), p. 46.

11. Genesis 6:6.

12. Jeremiah 18:13,15 NIV.

13. Abraham Heschel, *The Prophets,* vol. 1 (New York: Harper & Row, 1962), pp. 110-12.

14. Revelation 5:8.

15. Isaiah 49:15-16,23 NCV.

Chapter 7—Hope in the Eye of the Storm

1. Henri Nouwen, *Sabbatical Journey* (New York: Crossroad Publishing, 2000).

2. Andrew Solomon, *Noonday Demon* (New York: Simon & Schuster, 2002), p. 129-130.

3. Brennan Manning, *The Ragamuffin Gospel* (Sisters, OR: Multnomah Press, 2000), p. 31.

4. *Why Would a Good God Allow Suffering?* (Uhrichsville, OH: Barbour, 2001).

5. Psalm 13:1-3 NCV.

6. Psalm 34:18 NCV.

7. Psalm 32:8.

8. Isaiah 43:1-2,5,18-19 brackets in original.

9. C.S. Lewis, *Mere Christianity* (San Francisco: HarperSanFrancisco, 2001), p. 153.

10. Matthew 11:28-30, brackets and parentheses in original.

11. Manning, pp. 29-30.

Chapter 8—Permission for Prescriptions

1. Julie Barnhill, *Scandalous Grace* (Wheaton, IL: Tyndale, 2004), p. 100.

2. Frank Minirth and Paul Meier, *Happiness Is a Choice* (Grand Rapids, MI: Baker Books, 1994), pp. 163, 164.

3. Minirth and Meier, pp. 164, 165.

4. Renée Coates Scheidt, *Songs of the Night: Singing Sorrow's Songs Through the Darkness of Grief* (Friendswood, TX: Baxter Press, 2000), p. 26.

5. Scheidt, p. 28.

6. Scheidt, p. 53.

7. Scheidt, p. 79.

8. Scheidt, p. 61.

9. Barnhill, p. 99.

Chapter 9—Confessions of the Heart

1. Frank Minirth and Paul Meier, *Happiness Is a Choice* (Grand Rapids, MI: Baker, 1994), p. 98.

2. Mike Mason, *Champagne for the Soul* (Colorado Springs, CO: Waterbrook Press, 2003).

3. Luci Freed, *A Season to Heal* (Nashville, TN: Thomas Nelson, 1996).

4. Julie Barnhill, *Scandalous Grace* (Wheaton, IL: Tyndale, 2004), p. 100.

5. Frederick Buechner, *Now and Then* (San Francisco: HarperSanFrancisco, 1991).

6. Frederick Buechner, *Wishful Thinking* (San Francisco: HarperSanFrancisco, 1993).

7. Philippians 4:6-7, brackets and parentheses in original.

8. "FAX of Life," 12/02, www.faithmatters.com.

9. James 5:16 NCV.

10. Tim LaHaye, *How to Win over Depression* (Grand Rapids, MI: Zondervan, 1996).

11. Marilyn Ludolf, *Freed by Faith* (Kaleidoscope Publishers, 1995).

12. Miguel de Unamo, *In the Pursuit of Happiness* (Colorado Springs, CO: NavPress, 1996).

13. Philip Yancey, *Reaching for the Invisible God* (Grand Rapids, MI: Zondervan, 2002).

Chapter 10—Unlikely Cousins: Anger and Forgiveness

1. Frank Minirth and Paul Meier, *Happiness Is a Choice* (Grand Rapids, MI: Baker, 1994).

2. See John 2:12-16.

3. See Matthew 15:7-9.

4. Isaiah 29:13, brackets in original.

5. Ephesians 4:26, parentheses in original.

6. See John 13:4-5.

7. Paul Gilbert, *Overcoming Depression* (New York: Oxford University Press, Inc., 2001).

8. Marilyn Ludolf, *Freed by Faith* (Kaleidoscope Publishers, 1995).

9. See John 4:10-14.

Chapter 11—Fasten Your Seatbelts—This Ride Turns Over

1. Isaiah 60:1 brackets and parentheses in original.

2. Isaiah 60:5 brackets in original.

3. As quoted in the notes to *The Amplified Bible.*

Chapter 12—Bridge over Chaos—1

1. Henry Cloud and John Townsend, *Boundaries* (Grand Rapids, MI: Zondervan, 2002).

2. Paul Gilbert, *Overcoming Depression* (New York: Oxford University Press, Inc., 2001).

3. Cloud and Townsend.

4. Cloud and Townsend.

5. Tim LaHaye, *How to Win over Depression* (Grand Rapids, MI: Zondervan, 1996).

Chapter 13—Bridge over Chaos—2

1. Wayne Muller, *Sabbath* (New York: Bantam Books, 2000), p. 85.

2. As quoted in Muller, p. 55.

3. Linda Dillow, *Calm My Anxious Heart* (Colorado Springs, CO: NavPress, 1998), p. 26.

4. Tim LaHaye, *How to Win over Depression* (Grand Rapids, MI: Zondervan, 1996), p. 156.

5. Philippians 4:13-14.

6. Zephaniah 3:17.

7. Jeremiah 29:11.

8. 2 Corinthians 10:5, brackets and parentheses in original.

9. Brennan Manning, *Ruthless Trust* (San Francisco: HarperSanFrancisco, 2002), p. 37.

10. Paul Gilbert, *Overcoming Depression* (New York: Oxford University Press, Inc., 2001), p. 210.

11. Brennan Manning, *Reflections for a Ragamuffin* (San Francisco: HarperSanFrancisco, 1998), p. 366.

12. See *Journal of the American Geriatrics Society,* March 2005.

Chapter 14—Resurrected Heart

1. Sinclair Ferguson, *Daniel* (Nashville, TN: Word Publishing, 1993), p. 44.

2. Oswald Chambers, *My Utmost for His Highest,* December 25, 1 John 1:7 (Uhrichsville, OH: Discovery House Publishers, 1997), p. 34.

3. Luci Freed, *A Time to Heal* (Nashville, TN: Cumberland House, 1996).

4. Mike Mason, *Champagne for the Soul* (Colorado Springs, CO: Waterbrook, 2003).

5. Frederick Buechner, *The Hungering Dark* (New York: Harper & Row, 1989), p. 16.

6. "One Storm"/"The Deep," 2002; Travis Cottrell/Michael Mellett. Permission granted First Hand Revelation Music/Integrity/The Loving Company.

ABOUT THE AUTHOR

~

Bonnie Keen is a founding member of the recording trio First Call. Presently, she is a keynote speaker and vocalist, appearing at conferences and special events. Her three books include *Blessed Are the Desperate*,* *God Loves Messy People*,* and *A Ladder out of Depression*. She shares music from two solo CDs: *Marked for Life* and *God of Many Chances*.

Her passionate goal is to spark the reality of faith in others by sharing her personal journey of hope through song, books, laughter, and interactive video work. She is married to Brent King and has two children, Courtney and Graham. They live on a farm in western Tennessee.

For further information, please visit www.bonniekeen.com.

* Please contact the author for availability of these two books.

More Help and Resources
From Harvest House Publishers

Becoming Who God Intended
David Eckman

Whether you realize it or not, your imagination is filled with *pictures* of reality. The Bible indicates these pictures reveal your true "heart beliefs"—the beliefs that actually shape your everyday feelings and reactions to family, friends, and others, to life's circumstances, and to God.

David Eckman compassionately shows you how to allow God's Spirit to build new, *biblical* pictures in your heart and imagination. As you do this, you will be able to accept God's acceptance of you in Christ, break free of negative emotions and habitual sin…and finally experience the life God the Father has always intended for you.

"David Eckman is a man you can trust…His teaching resonates with God's wisdom and compassion."

Stu Weber, author of *Tender Warrior* and *Four Pillars of a Man's Heart*

∽

From Faking It to Finding Grace
Connie Cavanaugh

Spiritual dryness and disillusionment—nobody ever talks about them. But the truth is, almost every believer experiences periods of dry faith or feeling disconnected from God. Sadly, nearly everyone stays quiet about their doubts, and they feel alone at a time when they need support more than ever.

Connie Cavanaugh, featured columnist for *HomeLife* magazine, breaks the silence. Because she speaks out of her own ten-year struggle, you can trust her to help lead you toward a deeper and more mature friendship with God. Compassionately, she says,

- "You may feel empty and alienated, but you're not alone in this."
- "Don't try to get back to where you think you once were. Look ahead instead of back."
- "Get ready to listen to the Father, who's never stopped loving you."
- "Hold on to hope—He's calling you back."